"For years, when students have asked me, 'What's the one children's ministry book that I should read first?' I couldn't recommend just one. Instead, I recommended three: one about organization, one about teaching, and one about keeping children safe. Now I can recommend just one to read first because Jared Kennedy has managed to fit all of those essential elements into a single book!"

Timothy Paul Jones, C. Edwin Gheens Professor of Christian Family Ministry, The Southern Baptist Theological Seminary; author, *Family Ministry Field Guide*

"*Keeping Your Children's Ministry on Mission* delivers as advertised. Kennedy rightly knows that the gospel is the only means by which we will have a lasting impact on the next generation. To this thesis Kennedy adds a wealth of practical help and instruction to guide your ministry. Every senior pastor and children's ministry director should read this book and get it into the hands of all their teachers, helpers, and parents."

Marty Machowski, family pastor; author, *Build on Jesus*, *The Ology*, and *WonderFull*

"I can't think of a ministry in the church more complex than children's ministry, and I can't think of a better guide through that complexity than *Keeping Your Children's Ministry on Mission*. Whether you've worked with kids for days or years, you'll find this book comprehensive (from abuse policies to age-graded teaching), balanced (holding onto what's biblically ideal and practically realistic), and immediately helpful. Jared has packed more than a decade of experience and breadth of perspective into ten short chapters. It's like having your own children's ministry consultant only a shelf away."

Champ Thornton, Associate Pastor, Ogletown Baptist Church; author, *The Radical Book for Kid* and *Wonders of His Love: Finding Jesus in Isaiah*

"Are you passionate for kids to embrace the good news about Jesus and follow him throughout life? In this outstanding resource, Jared Kennedy offers us an essential biblical vision and engaging strategic plan to pursue Christ-exalting child and youth discipleship at church and home."

> **Barbara Reaoch,** Former Director of the Children's Division, Bible Study Fellowship International; author, *A Better Than Anything Christmas*

"What truly happens when the gospel shapes our goals for children's ministry? Jared Kennedy knows. As a studied pastor-practitioner, Jared understands how to help leaders and churches connect the gospel to the nuts and bolts—policy-making, recruiting, training, protecting, and reproducing—of children's ministry. If that's your mission, you have your manual!"

> **Dave Harvey,** President, Great Commission Collective; author, *I Still Do!*

"In *Keeping Your Children's Ministry on Mission*, Jared Kennedy provides a richly theological, accessible, and practical resource that is not only instructional but intriguing to read. This book written by an experienced family pastor is a sure guide for churches equipping servant leaders to make disciples for the next generation."

> **Jamaal Williams,** Lead Pastor, Sojourn Church Midtown; President, Harbor Network

"Many Christians groan about the future of the church instead of realizing the future is in their children's ministries. Kennedy not only reminds us about how foundational children's ministries can be in building God's Kingdom, but he also provides a practical guide for everything from how to keep children safe to how to teach gospel-centered lessons. Churches that follow his counsel will not only thrive now as families are strengthened, but will also invest in their own future."

> **Brian J. Arnold,** President, Phoenix Seminary

"Reading Jared Kennedy's *Keeping Your Children's Ministry on Mission* took me back to all the Sundays I've spent on my hands and knees in the nursery, passing out snacks in children's church, or teaching kids to sing God's praises. As theologically rich as it is practical, Kennedy guides us from the early church fathers through the roots of the Sunday school movement to contemporary protocols that safeguard the most vulnerable among us. Along the way, he casts a vision for children's ministry that welcomes children to their Savior and helps them find their place in God's family. As both a mother and a children's ministry worker for almost three decades, I heartily recommend it."

> **Hannah Anderson**, author; *Humble Roots: How Humility Grounds and Nourishes Your Soul* and *Turning of Days: Lessons from Nature, Season, and Spirit*

"Jared has labored in the trenches of children's ministry for years. You can tell by the wisdom that's dripping off of every page. If you work with children, do yourself a favor and read *Keeping Your Children's Ministry on Mission* from cover to cover. You'll be encouraged, challenged, and reoriented around the gospel of God's marvelous grace."

> **Deepak Reju**, Pastor of Biblical Counseling and Family Ministry, Capitol Hill Baptist Church; coauthor, *Build on Jesus: A Comprehensive Guide to Gospel-Based Children's Ministry*

"What a treasure this book is! It's jam-packed with biblical wisdom and relies richly on church history, which makes it a deeply edifying read for anyone concerned with the nurture of the next generation for Christ. It is immensely practical, with helpful illustrations to illuminate how the theory translates practically into ministry among children and families. It's clear that Jared is a seasoned practitioner with the critical ability to think theologically about ministry methodology. That's exactly the kind of person I want to train others for ministry and why I'll be recommending this book to all those striving to develop and direct Christ-centered, robust children's ministries."

> **Melanie Lacy**, Executive Director, Growing Young Disciples

Keeping Your Children's Ministry on Mission

Practical Strategies for
Discipling the Next Generation

Jared Kennedy

WHEATON, ILLINOIS

Library of Congress Cataloging-in-Publication Data

Names: Kennedy, Jared, 1978– author.
Title: Keeping your children's ministry on mission: practical strategies for discipling the next generation / Jared Kennedy.
Description: Wheaton, Illinois: Crossway, 2022. | Series: The gospel coalition | Includes bibliographical references and index.
Identifiers: LCCN 2021015134 (print) | LCCN 2021015135 (ebook) | ISBN 9781433576874 (trade paperback) | ISBN 9781433576881 (pdf) | ISBN 9781433576898 (mobipocket) | ISBN 9781433576904 (epub)
Subjects: LCSH: Church work with children. | Christian education of children. | Discipling (Christianity)
Classification: LCC BV639.C4 K46 2022 (print) | LCC BV639.C4 (ebook) | DDC 259/.2–dc23
LC record available at https://lccn.loc.gov/2021015134
LC ebook record available at https://lccn.loc.gov/2021015135

For the children's ministry leaders and volunteers
of the Harbor Network churches.

"They are the excellent ones, in whom
is all [the Savior's] delight."

Contents

Introduction

YEARS AGO, I attended a family-ministry conference. At the end of the event, the keynote speakers sat on a panel to discuss the state of family ministry. There was one moment during that discussion I'll never forget. The moderator looked at one of the panelists, a pastor named Steve Wright, and asked, "How can we make our children's and youth ministries more family centered?"

Steve sat quietly for a moment and then answered, "We shouldn't."

Everyone was stunned. This conference was designed to help leaders equip parents to disciple their kids. We all assumed—at least I did—that the goal was to orient our ministries around the family.

Steve allowed his answer to sink in before continuing, "We should be concerned about centering our children's and youth ministries around Jesus. That's what will aim our families in the right direction."

The Bible is clear about the responsibility that *both* parents *and* the believing community have to pass on our faith to the next generation (Deut. 6:6–9; Ps. 78:1–8). But in spite of that clarity, there are many different approaches to family discipleship. Some church leaders, like those of us who were shocked by Steve's response at the conference, have put their hope in parents as the primary faith trainers for the next generation. Others have been more jaded about parents' willingness to take up this mantle without help. As a result, they've put an emphasis upon the church's educational ministry, whether that's through schools, parachurch ministries, Sunday schools, or youth and children's ministries within the church.

But whatever our philosophy, Steve's comment points to an even bigger problem: a temptation to let the trappings of doing ministry with excellence keep us from seeing where the real glory is.

When leading local church children's ministry, I've experienced this temptation practically. I've let the un-mopped floor, the stalled check-in computer, and the missing activity sheet stress me out. While it's not a bad thing to want to welcome families to our church with warm hospitality, there are times when my worry over doing children's ministry well has revealed a misplaced faith. The level of anxiety I feel reveals that I'm trusting my hard work or the glitz and glam of attractional programming instead of trusting in Christ and the gospel. That's where our strategy for children's ministry must be centered.

Knowing Nothing Except Jesus

The apostle Paul stands in stark contrast to the way we tend to operate. In his letters to the Corinthian church, Paul gives us his vision for courageous, gospel-centered ministry—the kind of ministry that finds strength even in the midst of weakness. We find one of the best summaries of this theme in 1 Corinthians 1:31–2:5:

> It is written, "Let the one who boasts, boast in the Lord." And I, when I came to you, brothers, did not come proclaiming to you the testimony of God with lofty speech or wisdom. For I decided to know nothing among you except Jesus Christ and him crucified. And I was with you in weakness and in fear and much trembling, and my speech and my message were not in plausible words of wisdom, but in demonstration of the Spirit and of power, so that your faith might not rest in the wisdom of men but in the power of God.

Today, we admire the apostle for his missionary focus and the way he suffered for the sake of Christ. But Paul found it necessary to defend his apostleship against the charges of some vocal opponents. I love how Jack Klumpenhower describes the difference between Paul and his detractors in the Corinthian church:

> Corinth was a stopping point for traveling sages who spouted wisdom about personal success and religious insight. But Paul would not be one of them. His message about the cross of Christ was so superior that he spoke it plainly—weakly, he says, with trembling. He let the cross itself do the talking.[1]

While many of his hearers would have been tempted to think he lacked wisdom and had flunked out of Communications 101, Paul was confident that he had enough for ministry because he had the message of the cross.

I believe there are at least four ways the simple gospel message shapes our goals for children's ministry, and we can see each of them present in Paul's affirmation in 1 Corinthians 1:31–2:5. First, the gospel *seasons our hospitality* with humility; we don't come to children with lofty speech but with humble and full hearts, boasting only in the Lord. Second, the gospel *centers our teaching* on Jesus Christ and him crucified. All else pales in comparison to the central place of this message. Third, the gospel *forms our discipleship*; we're intentional about training children, and we have confidence that the Spirit's goal is to grow kids in conformity with Christ's story. Finally, the gospel *fuels our mission* so that the next generation's faith does not rest in the wisdom of men but in the power of God.

Chart 0.1

How the Gospel Shapes Our Goals for Children's Ministry[2]

Hospitality	Teaching	Discipleship	Mission
Gospel-*Seasoned* Presence	Gospel-*Centered* Message	Gospel-*Formed* Identity	Gospel-*Fueled* Witness
We welcome children in Jesus's name.	The content of the message matters; it must be about Jesus.	The cross of Christ shapes the entire Christian life.	Risk-taking, courageous faith comes from God.

Keeping Your Children's Ministry on Mission unpacks this fourfold strategy for gospel-centered, missional children's ministry—a ministry that equips parents, ministry leaders, and volunteers to engage children, point them to Christ and the larger church community, and then send them on mission. In chapter 1, we'll unpack the gospel and its implications for kids and explore how this good news moves both parents and the church community to pursue the next generation. In chapter 2, we'll view the history of children's and family ministry and directly address the temptation to let cultural assumptions and ministry ideals eclipse the glory of the gospel. Then over this book's final eight chapters, I'll encourage you to do the following:

- *Create* **welcoming environments for building relationships with kids and families.** Welcoming environments are the front door of children's ministry. We show Jesus to kids through the way we practice hospitality. We want facilities that are kid-friendly and safe. We want to season our environments with humility, prayer, and dependence on the Lord.
- *Connect* **kids and families to Christ through gospel-centered Bible lessons.** After kids have stepped through our front door, we want them to see Jesus in what we teach. This means preparing creative and educationally excellent Bible lessons that connect kids to Christ.
- *Grow* **alongside families by helping them take next steps in their spiritual journeys.** After families become regular parts of our community, we want to encourage them along in their journey of faith. We must be intentional both to call kids to appropriate faith responses and to equip parents with resources and rhythms that will help them walk with their children on a journey of discipleship.
- *Go* **with kids and families, sending them out on gospel-fueled mission.** Growth for kids moves beyond their own discipleship.

Faith should move them to be ambassadors for Christ who love their neighbors and take the good news to the world.

My prayer for those who read this book is that your confidence will be rooted in the simple message of "Jesus Christ and him crucified." It was all Paul needed, and it's all we need as well.

As you dive into these chapters, trust that God's actions through Jesus Christ are also truly enough to make you strong for children's ministry. As we consider the one who welcomed children himself, know that the Savior and his good news is enough to keep you, and to keep your children's ministry on mission.

PART 1

A GOSPEL-CENTERED VISION FOR CHILDREN'S MINISTRY

Stop! Believe! Christ Sent Me.

Our Both-And *Mission to the Next Generation*

THERE'S A LEGEND about John the apostle that's tucked away in a book you may have never read, especially if you're a children's or student minister. Musty second-century sermon manuscripts aren't top-shelf reading material for those of us who spend our days shopping at Costco for Goldfish crackers, leading early morning discipleship at Chick-fil-A, sanitizing toys in the nursery, or ordering pizza for Wednesday night gatherings. But if you've missed this story, you've missed a treasure.

At the conclusion of one of his sermons, Clement of Alexandria provides a beautiful account of ministry to the next generation. The story begins shortly after John, the beloved and now elderly disciple, was released from prison on the isle of Patmos:

After the tyrant's death [likely Clement is referring to the Roman emperor, Domitian], John returned from the isle of Patmos to Ephesus and used to go, when asked, to neighboring Gentile districts to appoint pastors, reconcile churches, or ordain someone designated by the Spirit. Arriving at a city nearby [probably the city of Smyrna in modern-day Turkey], he settled disputes among the brethren and then, noticing a spirited youth of superior physique and handsome appearance, commended him to the appointed pastor with the words: "I leave this young man in your keeping with Christ as my witness."[1]

In his later years, John served the church as an itinerant preacher and traveling advisor. As a wise senior saint, John was also on the lookout for young talent. After finding a young man with some leadership potential, he commended the boy to the local pastor for training. Then, John returned to his home church, and the local pastor took the young man home, raised him, and when he had confessed faith, baptized him.

During Christ's earthly ministry, he made his heart for children clear (Matt. 18:1–6; 19:13–15). Though his disciples missed the point at first, Clement's story about John encourages us to believe they eventually came around. John, after all, was on the lookout for future leaders who would continue his ministry in the next generation. And if you picked up this book, I imagine this passion to see the next generation know, trust, and follow God's ways has been passed along to you too. Children's ministry exists so that kids might hear the good news about Jesus and follow him all their days.

Children Need the Good News

We can summarize the gospel story as a fourfold movement: creation, fall, redemption, and consummation. What does this storyline teach us about kids?

First, we discover that God *created* children for himself. Kids are fearfully and wonderfully made (Ps. 139:14). Their lives are imbued with the glory of a universe that reflects God's beauty; they've been endowed with imagination and an ability to think and know. A child's life has value because he or she is made in God's image (Gen. 1:26–27). As image-bearers, children are also made for worship. From childhood, every human is fashioned for giving praise. Our desire as Christians is to bring up a generation that is dazzled by God, captured by his world and his works and always talking about them to one another (Ps. 145:3–7).[2]

Second, our children are *fallen* and sinful. They inhabit a world marred by sin, abuse, suffering, and death; they feel its pain. "Sometimes, people talk about coming from dysfunctional families," writes Robert Plummer. "The reality is that, because of sin, we are all 'dysfunctional' at the deepest level."[3] You've probably seen that children's program where the wooly mammoth, vampire, monsters, aliens, and an overgrown canary have all invaded a side street in Manhattan. In his brilliance, Jim Henson took some of our greatest fears and made them cute and educational. The child-friendly terrors that live together on Sesame Street should remind us of the hidden reality of childhood. Children are glorious and beautiful gifts from God and yet within each child—behind the cuteness—there's a fallen heart that's twisted from the moment of conception.

More often than not, our kids act like the monsters that destroy poor Guy Smiley's stage set. Every child is a sinner. It can be difficult for us to shoot straight with kids about this, but even they need to be faced with the reality of their brokenness. Charles Spurgeon says it well:

> Do not flatter the child with delusive rubbish about his nature being good and needing to be developed. Tell him he must be born again. Don't bolster him up with the fancy of his own innocence, but show him his sin. Mention the childish sins to which he is prone, and pray the Holy Spirit to work conviction in his heart and conscience.[4]

Even kids exchange delight in God's glory for delight in the pleasures of the moment (Rom. 1:21; 3:23). Just think about what happens when kids are called away from their toys to bath time or bed. There is a battle for affections going on in kids' hearts. Yes, children need comfort, care, and a healing touch. But they also need honest correction, because it's only when kids see the terror of their sin that they'll see their need for redemption. We need to hear Spurgeon's warning: "Do not hesitate to tell the child his ruin; he will not else desire the remedy."[5]

Third, *redemption* comes for children through Jesus. Remember, Jesus himself said, "Let the children come to me. Don't stop them! For the kingdom of heaven belongs to those who are like these children" (Matt. 19:14 NLT). Jesus's rebuke of his friends who would've kept kids at a distance should inspire us to include children in the life of our church communities. We must call even the youngest children to faith. We need to help each child see that Christ is his or her only hope. Children need us to help them to look outside of themselves to the salvation Jesus offers.

Through vacation Bible school programs, many of us have been trained to emphasize the ABCs with kids: *admit* you are a sinner, *believe* in Jesus, and *confess* faith in Him. We find this pattern in Scripture (Rom. 10:9–10), and there's nothing wrong with it so long as we make clear that salvation isn't about what we do but about what Christ has done.[6] If we only talk to kids about what they should do, we run the risk of confusing or discouraging them. When a child becomes aware of personal sin, he may become introspective and worry, "Did I do enough? How can Jesus live in my heart when I still get so angry?" What Jesus has done for us is the most important thing—so much more important than what we do. He saves us; we don't save ourselves. We must teach kids to look to the forgiveness that comes as a result of Christ's substitutionary death.

Finally, in light of the coming *consummation*, our children are potential brothers and sisters in Christ. When we get to glory, the most enduring relational reality will be our relationship to the Savior (Matt. 22:30). To be embraced by God's redemption is to be adopted as God's child, gaining a new identity, which transcends every earthly status and relationship. Plummer describes it this way: "If our children stand beside us in eternity, it will not be as our children but as our blood-redeemed brothers and sisters (Rev. 7:9–12)."[7] But if our children are going to join us as brothers and sisters in glory, they must hear the gospel now.

Our *Both-And* Responsibility

John knew this, and that's why he left the newly converted young man in the care of the local pastor in Smyrna. Sadly, things didn't go as the old apostle had hoped. We don't know all the details. Clement just says that after the young man was saved and baptized, the pastor "relaxed his oversight." At that point, as Clement explains, things went sideways:

> Some idle and morally lax youths corrupted the young man with lavish entertainment and then took him with them when they went out at night to commit robbery or worse crimes. Soon, he joined them and like a stallion taking the bit in mouth, he dashed off the straight road and down the cliff. Renouncing God's salvation, he went from petty offenses to major crimes and formed the young renegades into a gang of bandits with himself as chief, surpassing them all in violence and bloody cruelty.[8]

How should we respond when a young person turns away from the faith? Certainly, the fallen youth bears responsibility. But can we say each prodigal is just a bad seed? That's what the pastor in Smyrna thought:

> Time passed, and some necessity having emerged, they send again for John. He, when he had settled the other matters on account of which he came, said, "Come now, O bishop, restore to us the deposit which I and the Savior committed to thee. . . . I demand the young man, and the soul of the brother."
>
> The old [bishop], groaning deeply, and bursting into tears, said, "He is dead."
>
> "How and what kind of death?"
>
> "He is dead," [the bishop] said, "to God. For he turned

wicked and abandoned, and at last a robber; and now he has taken possession of the mountain in front of the church, along with a band like him."[9]

The pastor in Smyrna adopts a blame-the-kid approach. As we'll see in a moment, the story makes clear this is wrong. But before we learn how the story ends, consider the assumption that John makes about the young man's faith. He sees it as a deposit that he and Christ have "committed to *thee*."

So who is it that is responsible for the faith of youth and children?

The kids in our children's ministry on an average Sunday are, by God's grace, the next generation of pastors, church planters, worship leaders, counselors, small group leaders, and parents; they're the next generation of Christians. And if you're a parent or a church member, the Bible says that teaching the gospel to these children is your responsibility:

[Things] that we have heard and known,
　　that our fathers have told us.
We will not hide them from their children,
　　but tell to the coming generation
the glorious deeds of the Lord, and his might,
　　and the wonders that he has done.
He established a testimony in Jacob
　　and appointed a law in Israel,
which he commanded our fathers
　　to teach to their children,
that the next generation might know them,
　　the children yet unborn,

and arise and tell them to their children,
> so that they should set their hope in God
and not forget the works of God,
> but keep his commandments. (Ps. 78:3–7)

This psalm reminds us how God, throughout Israel's history, had children in mind (cf. Deut. 6:7–9). God wanted Israel's children to remember what he'd done to rescue and save. He wanted them to remember his laws and commands. He wanted the kids to hope and trust in him. And God gave the responsibility for training kids in the faith to two distinct groups: to Israelite *parents* and to their *covenant community.*

God commanded Israel's "fathers to teach . . . their children" (Ps. 78:5). No one has more potential to influence a child's spiritual direction than her parents. No Sunday children's ministry will come close to mom or dad's level of influence. Family ministry leader Reggie Joiner once compared the number of hours an average parent spends with a child to the number his church ministry team spent with the kids in their care:

At best, with those who attended our church consistently, we would only have about forty hours in a given year to influence a child. . . . The same fourth-grader who would spend nearly four hundred hours playing video games and studying math would spend forty hours in our environments with our leaders and teachers. That same day we calculated another number that shocked us: the amount of time the average parent had to spend with their children. It was three thousand hours in a single year.[10]

Joiner's 3,000/40 ratio is stunning. Family discipleship will happen in planned moments when parents pull out a Bible storybook, and it will happen in unplanned moments when a child is heartbroken, and her parents give comfort. It's in living rooms and cars, at bedsides and the breakfast table when many kids will hear and see their most consistent presentation of the gospel.

But training the next generation isn't limited to homes. God's command for parents to teach their kids was given in the context of a *community* ("in Jacob . . . in Israel," Ps. 78:5). Christian parents won't fulfill their responsibility to be generational disciple makers unless fellow believers support them. Here are a few reasons why church ministry to children and students is necessary:

1. To surround young people with godly adults who can provide love and care, truth they can build their lives on, and a model to follow (1 Cor. 11:1; 1 Pet. 5:2).
2. To reinforce a biblical view of the world. A child will sometimes listen to a children's or youth ministry volunteer more fully even though he has consistently heard the same truth from his parent (2 Tim. 4:2).
3. Because the family hasn't been given the keys to the kingdom, the church has. Therefore, the church is needed to affirm the salvation of children, and it's the ultimate spiritual accountability for the family (Matt. 16:19).
4. To be a neutral third party when there is a major family conflict, serving as an impartial advisor between parents and kids (2 Cor. 5:18).
5. To connect believing young people with other Christians, who support, encourage, and keep them accountable (Heb. 10:25).

6. To provide opportunities for young people to use their gifts to serve (1 Corinthians 12).

7. Because the church fights for truth and sound doctrine. It protects families from being drawn away by false teaching (1 Tim. 3:15).

8. Because spiritual growth generally happens within the context of community (Eph. 4:11–16).[11]

Children and students benefit from the combined influences of godly parents *and* the discipleship ministries of their local church. If kids growing up in Christian homes need the larger church family, how much more is the church needed to reach out and model the gospel for children who do not have Christian parents (Matt. 19:14; 28:19–20)? That seemed to be the case with the young man in Smyrna. Even with the church on his side, the youth's life soon went downhill.

How should we respond when a young person in our care turns away from the faith? Is it a time for self-reflection? Should we ask, "What did we do wrong? Was there something missing in our children's and youth ministry model?" Perhaps. But I find John's response more challenging.

Your Mission: Sharing the Good News with Little Ones

John doesn't lament failed discipleship strategies. His response is more active:

> The apostle tore his clothing, beat his head, and groaned. "A fine guardian I left for our brother's soul! But get me a horse and someone to show me the way." He rode off from the church,

just as he was. When he arrived at the hideout and was seized by the outlaws' sentries, he shouted, "This is what I have come for: take me to your leader!"

When John approached and the young leader recognized him, the young man turned and fled in shame. But John ran after him as hard as he could, forgetting his age, and calling out, "Why are you running away from me child—from your own father, unarmed and old? Pity me child, don't fear me! I will give account to Christ for you and, if necessary, gladly suffer death and give my life for yours as the Lord suffered death for us. Stop! Believe! Christ sent me."[12]

As soon as he heard about the straying son, this eighty-year-old minister mounted a horse and rode into the mountains to chase him down! It reminds me of what our Lord taught us in Matthew 18:10–14:

See that you do not despise one of these little ones. For I tell you that their angels in heaven always see the face of my Father in heaven. What do you think? If a man owns a hundred sheep, and one of them wanders away, will he not leave the ninety-nine on the hills and go to look for the one that wandered off? And if he finds it, truly I tell you, he is happier about that one sheep than about the ninety-nine that did not wander off. In the same way your Father in heaven is not willing that any of these little ones should perish. (NIV)

What can motivate an old pastor to chase down a rebellious teen in this way? Only a conviction that he himself had once been the wandering lamb whom the Savior had pursued. As John wrote in one of his letters: "We love because he first loved us" (1 John 4:19).

Clement tells us that the young gang leader "stopped, stared at the ground, threw down his weapons, and wept bitterly." He flung his arms around the old apostle and begged for mercy. John assured him that he'd found forgiveness from the Savior, and upon the young man's repentance, the Father rejoiced!

Brothers and sisters who serve in children's or youth ministry, this is your mission. The Savior has pursued and found you. Now you have the privilege of carrying the good news to little ones, and persevering with them throughout their lives. Remember John the apostle's example the next time you're stacking piles of cotton balls for a preschool craft or playing knockout with middle school boys. Allow this good news to move you to action, and call the kids in your care to believe, because Christ sent you!

Keeping Your Children's Ministry on Mission is meant to inspire and encourage you in the task of reaching and discipling the next generation with the gospel. I also want to give you a clear strategy for that task. But, as this book's title suggests, it's easy to get distracted from our simple commission. The truth is, we all come into ministry with experiences and assumptions that form our expectations about what a children's ministry should be. So, before I begin unpacking a strategy for gospel-centered children's ministry, let's look at history and think about how today's children's ministry came about.

2

Knowing What We Shouldn't Do

*Warnings from the History
of Family Ministry*

MY GRANDPARENTS once had a wall of pictures in the long hallway at the top of the stairs in their home. I can remember my mom and aunts standing around the pictures after a new cousin was born, talking about how much the new addition favored one older relative or another. These days it seems like everyone is tracing their ancestry and genetic history. Discovering where we've come from helps us to understand something about ourselves.

That's one of the reasons I love Martin Luther. He's like a bombastic German uncle who has helped me to understand both the centrality of the gospel and our *both-and* responsibility for family discipleship. Luther's plan for reaching the next generation began with a focus on the family. He was passionate about parents teaching their children.[1]

During the Middle Ages, professional clergy and church institutions such as schools and monasteries had taken pride of place in the role of passing down the faith. But with the dawn of the Reformation, church leaders called for a return to family discipleship, instructing parents, and especially fathers, to take an active role in discipling their children.[2] Luther led the way. When giving his lectures on the book of Genesis, the Reformer famously compared the Christian home to a school and a church:

> Abraham had in his tent a house of God and a church, just as today any godly and pious head of a household instructs his children . . . in godliness. Therefore, such a house is actually a school and a church, and the head of the household is a bishop and priest in his house.[3]

Luther helped to move the church from a culture of clericalism to a culture where the work of *every* believer mattered. The Wittenberg pastor believed that the ordinary labors of life—everything from laboring at a trade to changing a baby's diapers—are charged with meaning. In one sermon, Luther rebuked men who might avoid marriage because of the dirty work involved in raising children.[4] He was convinced that God is always at work in our labors at home, no matter how ordinary they are. Luther was also "confident in the power of the gospel rightly preached to move hearts and generate energy for its cause."[5] He believed that gospel preaching would move fathers to become disciple-makers within their homes.

This conviction never wavered. However, Luther's experience visiting the churches of rural Saxony in the late 1520s seems to have convinced him of the need for stronger institutional safeguards as well. After the visits, Luther wrote:

> Good God, what wretchedness I beheld! The common people, especially those who live in the country, have no knowledge whatever of Christian teaching, and unfortunately many pastors are quite incompetent and unfitted for teaching. Although the people are supposed to be Christian, are baptized, and receive the holy sacrament, they do not know the Lord's Prayer, the Creed, or the Ten Commandments, they live as if they were pigs and irrational beasts.[6]

After seeing such depressing conditions, Luther prepared a catechism that could be taught *both* in homes *and* in church-sponsored schools.[7] He became convinced that parents couldn't train up their children alone. They needed support from the church community.

Reaching the Youth Culture for Christ

In many ways, the story of our contemporary family ministry movement mirrors Luther's journey.

In 1844, the Young Men's Christian Association (the YMCA) was founded in London to improve the lives of young working men; soon, churches followed this model by creating their own Young People's Associations or Christian Endeavor Societies.[8] Those were early precursors to contemporary youth ministry.

But if you ask me, I'd trace today's student and children's ministry models back to the 1940s and 1950s. During the latter half of the twentieth century, the social function of the adolescent years began to change. The teenage years were no longer viewed as an intermediary life stage with adulthood as the goal but as a distinctive youth culture that resisted movement toward adulthood.[9]

In response, Christian leaders created organizations and ministries that sought to reach teenage culture for Christ. Parachurch ministries such as Young Life (1941) and Youth for Christ (1944) were quickly followed by age-directed youth ministry programs in local churches.[10] Youth ministry leaders of the 1970s, 1980s, and 1990s saw the youth culture as their mission field. They set up drum sets, used lights and video, and played crazy Nickelodeon-style *Double Dare* games as a way of becoming "all things to all people that by all means [they] might save some" (1 Cor. 9:22).

But the youth ministry movement of the late 1900s also had its liabilities. What emerged was a segmented-programmatic approach that comprehensively divided up a congregation according to age and special interest. In this compartmentalized model, youth groups—and sometimes children's ministries—developed their own expressions of Christian community that operated in isolation from the rest of the congregation. These groups typically rejected older forms of worship such as hymn singing, and the youth ministry leaders would pursue their own methods and teaching plans that were disconnected from the direction—and sometimes even the theology—of the larger church.

Another disadvantage of the programmatic youth ministry model was a growing sense among some parents that they themselves would never be able to reach their children. They needed younger, cooler youth leaders who were, one might say, "in touch with kids today." During the Reformation, Luther had fought

TWO DANGERS OF SEGMENTED-PROGRAMMATIC MINISTRY

Segmented-Programmatic Ministry comprehensively divides up the congregation according to age and special interest, delegating the discipleship of the next generation to specialized ministers who oversee church programs. The two dangers are:

Segmented Ministry Silos—Kids and youth ministry become compartmentalized expressions of Christian community and are disconnected from the faith of older generations.

The Drop-Off Mentality—Parents assume that the responsibility for training their children spiritually is best left with professionals.

against the clergy-laity divide within the Roman Catholic church. But less than five hundred years later, many parents assumed the responsibility for evangelizing and training their children was best left with professionals. Here's how Timothy Paul Jones describes this drop-off mentality: "School teachers are perceived as the persons responsible to grow the children's minds, coaches are employed to train children's bodies, and specialized ministers at church ought to develop their souls."[11]

Bringing Student Discipleship Back Home

Thankfully, just as it did during the Reformation, the church has once again responded to an overemphasis on *segmented* and *institutional* ministry. In the late 1990s and early 2000s, a group of family ministry leaders arose and registered their concerns about both of these trends. These leaders formed what has come to be known as the family ministry movement, and they've proposed a number of creative alternatives to programmatic youth ministry.

Proponents of *family-based* ministry, for instance, have added intergenerational and parent-training activities to their churches' existing age-organized activities. The goal of these supplemental events and learning experiences is to draw the generations together.[12]

Family-integrated churches are more radical. They've eliminated age-graded classes and events altogether. There's no youth group, children's ministry, or senior adult programs in these churches. The generations learn and worship together, and parents bear the primary responsibility for the evangelism and discipleship of their children.[13]

Many churches found an approach between the supplemental family-based model and the extreme of family-integrated churches. Adopting what has come to be known as the *family-equipping model*, these church leaders have sought to coordinate a church's age-stratified ministry structures and the parents' ministry to their children at home around "a master plan to build faith and character in their sons and daughters."[14]

While the solutions proposed by these scholars and practitioners varied, they shared two common goals: (1) de-compartmentalizing the church's people by reconnecting church and home, and (2) empowering parents as the primary faith-trainers for the next generation.

Chart 2.1

The Mathematics of the Family Ministry Movement[15]

$\div$ **Segmented-Programmatic Ministry** comprehensively *divides* up the congregation according to age and special interest, delegating the discipleship of the next generation to specialized ministers who oversee church programs.

$+$ **Family-Based Ministry** *adds* intergenerational and parent-training activities to existing age-organized activities. The congregation maintains youth ministry, children's ministry, senior adult ministry, etc., but events and learning experiences are planned to draw the generations together.

$-$ **Family-Integrated Ministry** is by far the most radical. This approach *subtracts* all age-graded classes and events. There is no youth group, no children's ministry, and no age-graded training programs. The generations learn and worship together, and parents bear the primary responsibility for the evangelism and discipleship of their children.

$\times$ **Family-Equipping Ministry** *multiplies* the impact of age-stratified structures by transforming activities and events so that they train parents, involve the generations, and equip the congregation with resources to disciple the next generation.

Is There Something Wrong with Focusing on the Family?

I'd consider myself an advocate for the family ministry movement. After all, God has a heart for each successive generation, and I know kids and students benefit from the combined influences of loving parents and a missional church community. But as I've worked with kids and families over the past fifteen years, I've had some experiences that, like Luther after his trip to Saxony, have tempered my enthusiasm. I'm concerned in particular that our ideals about how to do family discipleship have sometimes distracted us from our more primary responsibility to teach kids the gospel.

Here are a couple of the ways we get distracted.

First, we're tempted to believe that getting family discipleship right will automatically produce Christian kids. In the early days of the family ministry movement, you'd hear a lot of daunting statistics about church kids leaving the faith after they went off to college. Many leaders offered new family-discipleship strategies to the church as a way of helping to raise retention rates.[16] It makes sense, doesn't it? We want our kids to stay connected to Christ as they grow older. We'd like to have surefire strategies for keeping young men from running off into the hills with a gang of bandits.

But the danger with promoting strategies is that we sometimes overpromise. If we give the impression that getting your family-discipleship strategy right is the way to produce perfect, Christian children, then we're presenting a false gospel. It's a subtle form of legalism, one that pastor Dave Harvey calls the "false hope of deterministic parenting."[17]

Don't get me wrong. I believe Christian parents should be expectant about their kids' future. Our children are raised in homes and churches where they hear the gospel taught (1 Cor. 7:14). They've been given the opportunity to taste and see that the Lord is good (Ps. 34:8). But there's no formula for ensuring our kids will persevere as Christians. Both parents and family ministry workers must be clear that our responsibility is to faithfully teach the good news to the next generation and then leave the results to the Lord. Salvation is his work. Practicing family devotions or disciplining consistently can't prevent kids from rebelling. Remember, our perfect Father has prodigal children (Luke 15:11–32). What right do we have to assume that wandering can't be a part of our own children's stories?[18] Being more honest about this will release the parents we're shepherding from unnecessary guilt and encourage them to build home environments where older kids who wander spiritually will be welcomed back into the fold.

Second, we're tempted to let promoting our family ministry ideals eclipse the priority of reaching the lost. The family ministry movement as a whole emphasizes the importance of parents as the primary faith-trainers for their children. This is in fact biblical (Deut. 6:1–12; Ps. 78:1–8). But what about kids whose parents are absent, unbelieving, or just immature? Kevin Jones writes:

> I have served in contexts where the *worst* person to discern the condition of a child's heart is the parent! Parents can be toxic, enabling, and spiritually damaging to the growth and development of young believers. In the best cases, fathers and mothers are present spiritually—but the best case doesn't always describe the contexts where God has placed us. In some situations, the parent may be one of the reasons a young Christian struggles to grow spiritually.[19]

I've seen friends and church leaders advocate for sweeping changes both in their church communities and the church at large in the name of a family ministry ideal. Earlier, I told you how family-integrated churches reacted radically to programmatic and segmented ministry. One thing I love about this approach is the emphasis it puts on exposing young people to cross-generational church life; this is essential for kids' growth.[20] However,

TWO DANGERS OF FOCUSING ON THE FAMILY

The False Gospel of Deterministic Parenting—We're tempted to believe that getting family discipleship right will automatically produce Christian kids.

Creating Gospel-Preventing Social Barriers—We're tempted to let promoting our family ministry ideals eclipse the priority of reaching the lost.

promoting our family-discipleship hobbyhorse should never eclipse the priority of the Great Commission (Gal. 2:11–14).

Kids trained from an early age might pull off sitting through a long-winded sermon without rolling matchbox cars down the wooden pews, but will unchurched visitors and new believers be as successful?[21] In our pursuit of family-ministry ideals, we must be careful not to create social barriers to the gospel.

As we pursue ways that our churches can experience intergenerational family life, we also need ministry approaches that remember kids from unbelieving homes and that capitalize on the pedagogical advantage of age-directed lessons (see chapter 7). Think about it. Why should we have young children sit all the way through a sermon they don't understand? Even within the Bible, there seem to be some parts—Song of Songs, for example—that should be taught publicly (2 Tim. 3:16–17) but seem to be reserved for adults and older teens, not for younger children (Song 8:4). Other parts of the Bible, such as Proverbs, are geared toward youth (Prov. 1:8; cf. Ps. 119:9–16)! We have

Chart 2.2

Potential Dangers of the Family Ministry Movement Models

Segmented-Programmatic Ministry
Because each generation's expression of faith is compartmentalized, inter-generational influence can be lost. Moreover, there can be a tendency for Christian parents to see ministry leaders as the professionals who are primarily responsible for discipling their kids.

Family-Based Ministry
While family events are planned, the strategy for equipping Christian parents to lead in family discipleship can sometimes be less clear. It's also unclear whether the drop-off mentality and mindset of viewing ministry leaders as professional faith-trainers has been adequately addressed.

Family-Integrated Ministry
There is a narrow focus on churched families—on the church as a family of families—and this family ministry ideal can eclipse the church's missionary purpose—to reach the lost. The family-integrated model narrowly applied fails to engage the broader daycare culture and to reach youth and children whose parents are not believers.

Family-Equipping Ministry
The intentional focus on equipping parents can at times be alienating to families who are not from a Christian background. Furthermore, when this and other family ministry models have been presented as ways to counter the church's low retention emphasis, one can get the false impression that getting family discipleship right will automatically produce Christian kids; that's the false gospel of deterministic parenting.

to keep our priorities in order. The church's goal in discipling the next generation is not to train kids so they can sit quietly through church services. Our goal is for them to hear about the Savior and, by God's grace, be changed by him.

Chart 2.3

How the Gospel Shapes Our Goals for Children's Ministry

Hospitality	Teaching	Discipleship	Mission
Gospel-*Seasoned* Presence	Gospel-*Centered* Message	Gospel-*Formed* Identity	Gospel-*Fueled* Witness
We welcome children in Jesus's name.	The content of the message matters; it must be about Jesus.	The cross of Christ shapes the entire Christian life.	Risk-taking, courageous faith comes from God.

As you continue through this book, we'll move from evaluating the history of family ministry toward working out a gospel-centered ministry strategy. I believe there are at least four ways the gospel shapes our goals for children's ministry. It shapes our hospitality, teaching, discipleship, and mission (see chart 2.3). Over the next eight chapters, I'll unpack each of these key areas and encourage you to:

- *Create* welcoming environments for building relationships with kids and families.
- *Connect* kids and families to Christ through gospel-centered Bible lessons.
- *Grow* alongside families by helping them take next steps in their spiritual journey.
- *Go* with kids and families, sending them out on gospel-fueled mission.

I have confidence in these strategies and methods. I think they're biblical and important, but I also hope I'm sober enough not to overpromise results. These strategies aren't silver bullets, and I don't mean for them to be understood that way. My goal in teaching these methods is to help you keep the mission—sharing the gospel with little ones—the main thing. God has called *both* parents *and* the church to partner for the sake of reaching the next generation. Ultimately, we're working together as a means to a greater end—seeing the next generation come to know and love Jesus.

Reflection on Part 1

A Gospel-Centered Vision
for Children's Ministry

AT THE END OF EACH SECTION of this book, I've included a set of questions for reflection and evaluation as well as a list of resources for further study. Before you move on, take time to think through these questions and reflect upon your ministry context.

Questions for Reflection and Evaluation

1. Read 1 Corinthians 1:31–2:5. What key truths stand out to you in this passage? How is your regular ministry mindset different from the vision for ministry Paul outlines here? What one thing would you change about your ministry to better embody this biblical model?

2. Even though parents are to pass on faith to their children (Deut. 6:1–12), we can idolize and idealize the family in ways that become barriers to the gospel. Is the tendency of parents in your church community to have a drop-off mentality—entrusting church professionals with the primary responsibility for teaching their children? Or do they tend to over-prioritize the family—thinking their personal values, practice of family discipleship, or educational choices will ensure their kids turn out right?

3. Review charts 2.1 and 2.2. Is there a particular family-ministry model to which you aspire? Why? What biblical support do you have for that approach? What do you think makes it the right choice for your ministry context? What potential liabilities does this approach carry with it?

After considering this, consider what others in your church would say—whether parents or leadership. Is there a particular family-ministry model with which your church most closely aligns? Be honest about where you are now. It's impossible to move toward your goals without first acknowledging your current reality.

For Further Study

Cimo, Pat and Matt Markins. *Leading KidMin: How to Drive Real Change in Children's Ministry*. Chicago: Moody, 2016.

Joiner, Reggie. *Think Orange: Imagine the Impact When Church and Family Collide*. Colorado Springs: David C. Cook, 2009.

Jones, Timothy Paul, et al. *Perspectives on Family Ministry*, 2nd ed. Nashville, TN: B&H Academic, 2019.

Machowski, Marty and Deepak Reju. *Build on Jesus: A Comprehensive Guide to Gospel-Based Children's Ministry*. Greensboro, NC: New Growth Press, 2021.

Michael, David. *Zealous: 7 Commitments for the Discipleship of the Next Generations*. Minneapolis: Truth78, 2020.

PART 2

CREATE WELCOMING
ENVIRONMENTS

3

Meeting Jesus at the Front Door

Welcoming and Including
Kids and Families

ONE DAY, Jesus's disciples came to him with a question: "Who is the greatest in the kingdom of heaven?" (Matt. 18:1). The parallel passage in Luke 9:46–48 reveals that the disciples had been debating among themselves as to which of them would be the greatest. It's as if each of Jesus's followers is asking, "Will it be me? Am *I* the one who is up for promotion?" How would you handle this group of overly ambitious, trainee ministers? Jesus responded to their self-indulgent question with two counter-cultural answers: *become like children and welcome them*.

For Jesus, welcoming children didn't start with having a multi-story jungle gym in the front lobby or a designated family entrance. It didn't even start with having good signage or smiling and greeting kids by name. For the Savior, welcoming children begins with taking the posture of a child. As the disciples stood and debated who would be the greatest in the kingdom of heaven, Jesus called over a child and stood him in the midst of his followers. Then he said, "Truly, I say to you, unless you turn and become like children, you will never enter the kingdom of heaven" (Matt. 18:3).

In Jesus's day, the Jewish people would have agreed with our own culture that biological and adoptive family relationships are vitally important. The Old Testament describes children as a heritage and reward from the Lord (Ps. 127:3). Children played a central role in God's promises to his people (Gen. 3:15; 12:2; 15:5).[1] On the other hand, the Jewish people did not romanticize children. There were no Gerber ads, Baby Gap stores, or baby-of-the-month calendars in first-century Palestine. Instead, Jewish literature of the time—including the Old Testament—realistically describes youth and children as immature and foolish, in need of consistent discipline and correction.[2]

What you never find in Jewish literature, as Judith Gundry Volf writes, "are children put forward as models for adults, and in a Greco-Roman setting [the occupying culture at the time], comparison with children was highly insulting."[3] So, when Jesus answered his apprentices by telling them they must become like kids to enter his kingdom, it would have certainly shocked them.

Maturity and wisdom come with age. Why go backwards? Here is the Savior's answer: "Whoever humbles himself like this child is the greatest in the kingdom of heaven. Whoever receives one such child in my name receives me" (Matt. 18:4–5). Jesus requires his disciples to take a childlike posture because of children's lowly and humble status.[4] "The child is held up as an ideal," writes

D. A. Carson, "not of innocence, purity, or faith, but of humility and unconcern for social status."[5] Jesus wants his disciples to be childlike because young kids don't pretend to have it all together. They poop and cry and get into things. Jesus wanted his team of disciples to see that they were just as needy, and he wants us to see it as well.

When I was a kid, I fell and knocked out my two front teeth. Now they're porcelain caps. One Saturday night more recently, I jarred one of the caps loose. To make matters worse, I'd been asked to lead a children's lesson during the church service the next morning. As I taught, one of the boys kept pointing and saying, "Mr. Jared, you've got a loose tooth!" He was right. And before the lesson was done, my front tooth fell out! Humbling moments like that one reveal I'm as big of a mess as the kids I'm leading. Truthfully, we need this perspective right from the start.

Like Jesus's first followers, Christian disciples today have a tendency to think we're the important ones! We've read gospel-centered books; we've learned discipleship skills; and we often have some level of status within a Christian community. You don't have to have thousands of Instagram followers to feel like you've made it. You don't need to win an award to think highly of yourself at the expense of others. But it's this tendency to fall into entitlement and pride that Jesus targets with his command to embrace the humility of a child. Jesus tells those who desire to be great that they must put down their regard for status altogether.

In *Mere Christianity*, C. S. Lewis writes about how even those who understand the command to be humble can drift toward self-regard:

Do not imagine that if you meet a really humble man he will be what most people call "humble" nowadays: he will not be a sort of greasy, smarmy person, who is always telling you that, of course, he is nobody. Probably all you will think about him is that he seemed a cheerful, intelligent chap who took a real interest in what you said to him. If you do dislike him, it will be because you feel a little envious of anyone who seems to enjoy life so easily. He will not be thinking about humility: he will not be thinking about himself at all.[6]

The prescription for those who think they are great is admitting their pride and then stooping to serve those who are lowly—in particular, says Jesus, "the little ones" (Matt. 18:10). That's what it looks like to have a life seasoned by the gospel. After all, Jesus embraced humility by stooping to serve his disciples (John 13:1–17; Phil. 2:1–11)—by stooping to serve us. Now we are called to love and serve the lowly just as he first loved us (1 John 4:19).

The Gospel's Call to Welcome Children

Children's ministry is one of the biggest challenges a church can face. There is so much to think about—facility, curriculum, check-in, security, recruiting and training a quality team, and of course, where to buy quality, odor-free diaper pails in bulk! It's hard to know where to begin. I've talked with pastors who have a clear vision for preaching and worship, but children's ministry befuddles them.

In my work with children's ministers, I've encouraged them to start by slowing down and giving kids and families the gift of their grace-filled presence. In other words, welcome kids in Jesus's

GOSPEL-SEASONED HOSPITALITY

Gospel-seasoned hospitality requires slowing down and giving kids and families the gift of our grace-filled presence. In other words, it means welcoming kids in Jesus's name.

name. Such gospel-seasoned hospitality involves three things: humble prayer, warm reception, and valuing children enough to build a relationship with them.

First, pray. Begin on your knees (Matt. 7:11; 18:3–4). If you work with children long enough—as a parent, a children's ministry worker, or a teacher—there will be days when the kids will bring you to your knees. But that's where we should have been all along: in a posture of prayer, calling out like a child. We've seen Christ's call to be humble like a child in Matthew 18:3–4, but Jesus had already taught his followers in the Sermon on the Mount about what childlike humility looks like practically; it involves childlike prayer. A baby cries out for milk before she even knows how to walk. A good parent answers the cry and meets the child's need. In Matthew 7:11, Jesus reminds us, "How much more will your Father who is in heaven give good things to those who ask him!"

Fletcher Lang serves as lead pastor at City on a Hill Church in Somerville, Massachusetts. I spoke with him about what it has looked like to establish a strong children's ministry culture in his new church. "Pray, pray, pray," he said. Fletcher is right. We can't do effective children's ministry unless God shows up. And we can't expect him to show up unless we humble ourselves, admit our need, and ask.

Prayer is the receptive, God-dependent posture of the gospel, and Christ wants that posture to season the atmosphere of our ministries. As we go to Christ in prayer, we can be confident that he will welcome us and lead us in turn to welcome families. This is the pattern we find in Hebrews 10:19–25:

> Therefore, brothers, since we have confidence to enter the holy places by the blood of Jesus, by the new and living way that he opened for us through the curtain, that is, through his flesh, and since we have a great priest over the house of God, let us draw near with a true heart in full assurance of faith, with our hearts sprinkled clean from an evil conscience and our bodies washed with pure water. Let us hold fast the confession of our hope without wavering, for he who promised is faithful. And let us consider how to stir up one another to love and good works, not neglecting to meet together, as is the habit of some, but encouraging one another, and all the more as you see the Day drawing near.

Hebrews 10 is more than just a passage about going to church and encouraging the others there. Being present with other people is a reality that's rooted in Christ's presence with us. Jesus has saved and sustains us by his flesh and blood. He washes us clean and welcomes us into his throne room. And because we've been welcomed into God's presence, we now can receive others with love, good works, and our faithful presence as well.

So, before you welcome the kids and families this week, grab another teacher or huddle together with the whole children's ministry team and go before God's throne. Begin with prayer.

Let the experience of being welcomed before God fuel your soul as you welcome children and families.

Second, open the door. Give kids and families a warm reception (Matt. 18:5). In *Making Your Children's Ministry the Best Hour of Every Kid's Week*, Sue Miller and David Staal write about their desire to create child-targeted children's ministry environments. They encourage children's ministry leaders to ask questions such as, "Are we doing the kinds of things children really enjoy? Are we singing the style of songs children want to sing? Are we teaching lessons children will understand? Would children invite lost friends here?" Their goal is for a girl or boy to experience their weekend Bible classes and think, "This is for me!"[7] It's a good thing for a church's children's ministry environment to be bright, playful, kid-friendly, and safe—the sort of place where kids will want to be. It's important to have adequate signage for new visitors, and if you use check-in technology, it helps to cultivate a good experience for moms and dads when your system is user-friendly and up-to-date.

But kid-friendly facilities and activities are merely a first step. It's also important to open the door for kids and families personally. Find a few parents who are passionate about your church's mission and vision. Invite them to stand in the reception area of your children's ministry each week and encourage them to build relationships with new families. Find a way to make these hospitality team members easily identifiable—with nametags, lanyards, or t-shirts. And when you're recruiting team members to open the front door of your children's ministry, look for individuals who are gifted at being outgoing and welcoming. You're not just looking for warm bodies; you're looking for *warm leaders*.

When Matt Friend, pastor of Bible Center Church in Charleston, West Virginia, teaches church ministry teams to provide a warm reception for children, he encourages them to remember three words: look, level, and love. Leaders should *look* for families that are new to the church as well as those who may be having a rough morning. Move toward these families and be intentional about interacting with their kids. Move down to the kids' *level* and show them *love* by asking and remembering their names and interests.

Small conversations are some of the most important parts of ministry. As Virginia Ward, Reggie Joiner, and Kristen Ivy observe, "That may be especially true when the conversation is about something that interests someone else."[8] Lingering and listening demonstrates to new families that you value them. Remembering what is shared with you and taking time to follow up after the visit with a personal thank-you note or a care package drives home the fact that you care and see kids and families as worth your time.

Third, value kids as a part of the community (Matt. 18:10, 12–14).[9] A consumer mindset often drives our society's approach to kids. Newlyweds sometimes don't want children because of the financial burden. Others naively think that having kids will fill a void in their lives. Seasoned parents by contrast might be tempted to say, "I pour so much into my kids. I can't wait until they get old enough to give something back." Even in ministry, we sometimes see children as a means to an end: "If you want to reach parents, you need to reach their children. If the kids don't like the church, the parents won't come back." But statements like these judge the value of children based on what can be gained *from* them.

LEARNING A CHILD'S NAME[10]

What would it take for you to get in the habit of learning and remembering the names of the kids in your local church? Here are five ideas.

1. Say the name out loud. When you are first told a name, immediately say it back. Say it again during conversation. Then, say it out loud a third time when you want to introduce another person into the conversation. A person serving in a hospitality ministry can say a new child's name at least three times before drop-off at the classroom is complete.

2. Pronounce the name correctly. Don't give up on this. Keep repeating it until you get it right. If a child has a name that differs from what's on your attendance sheet, go with "Bobby" instead of "Robert." If the pronunciation is challenging, ask for help. Pronouncing a child's name correctly communicates respect for their history, family, and culture.

3. Discover the name's story. If you really want to get personal, discover more about the story behind a child's name. You might hear a wildly fascinating story about great-aunt Florence. Or you may learn that the name has significant or even symbolic meaning.

4. Write the name down somewhere. Even if it's just with a crayon on the back of a craft or activity sheet, writing down a name can make it easier to remember. Also, log the child's name on your classroom roll sheet or a notecard where you can reference it occasionally.

5. Pray the name frequently. Praying privately for someone by name will influence the way you see that individual. Praying publicly for someone by name can influence how they see themselves. Consider creating a prayer calendar for the children in your ministry so that you can pray for a few kids each week.

Jesus sees it differently. Little ones are valuable to him. They must not be despised, because their angels see the face of the Father. The Savior doesn't want one child to perish (Matt. 18:10, 12–14). Jesus even goes so far as to say, "Whoever receives one such child in my name receives me" (18:5). For Jesus, valuing kids as a part of the community is essential.

Churches that practice infant baptism affirm children as part of the faith community in their confession.[11] Baptists like me and other evangelicals who emphasize the need to call children to believe before affirming them in the faith do not. But whatever our doctrinal stance on children as full-fledged covenant members of the church body, we must all reckon with how the New Testament speaks about kids.

Jesus tells us that a child's presence must not be despised or hindered, "for to such belongs the kingdom of heaven" (Matt. 19:14). The churches to which Paul wrote must have taken this to heart, because the apostle addresses children directly, expecting them to be present with the gathered community when his letters were read (Col. 3:20). Moreover, he addresses the children who were there as those who are "in the Lord" (Eph. 6:1), demonstrating an expectation that at least some of these young children were already included in Christ and could be expected to hear, believe, and obey God's word. Children aren't just missing out when they don't participate in the larger church community; the New Testament assumption is the church is missing out when children don't partake.

If we're to take the biblical record about children seriously, we must believe that their presence with the community of faith is vital. Robert J. Keeley describes a number of ways to include children in the life of a church fellowship. One of the most practical is by simply giving kids a real job to do. As he explains,

> Children and young people should participate in the life of the church through authentic tasks. By *authentic* I mean tasks in which they give as well as receive. They should feel that if they aren't doing their part, the whole group will suffer.[12]

Keeley goes on to describe a program at his church that gives some elementary-aged kids the opportunity to serve as candlelighters and one child each week the opportunity to march the Bible into the sanctuary at the beginning of the service and then take it out into the world at the end. He also explains how teenagers in his church are considered "regular citizens" who work in the nursery, play instruments in worship, and run the sound board.[13]

As I read Keeley's encouragements, I think about my childhood experience. In middle school, the guys in our youth group were regularly recruited by our church's deacons to help pass the offering plate. Those older men knew me by name, and I still remember them. I also thought about my oldest daughter and her friends who have served with our church's hospitality team, making coffee and passing out bulletins. When church leaders are mindful of the next generation as they plan worship services and other events, and youngsters serve side-by-side with adults, kids and youth grow up understanding their own value to the church community at large.

More importantly, when kids are given an opportunity to contribute to the life of the church during their growing-up years, they're building relationships with Christians who are ahead of them on their faith journey. These relationships are more important to a child's faith over the long haul than any child-targeted program or state-of-the-art youth ministry facility. Building relationships with kids shows that we truly value them. As Keeley writes, "It's when we *individually* take the time to get to know the kids in our own church that we can have the most impact on them *collectively*."[14]

How Quickly We Forget

Sometimes I think valuing children the way Jesus did can be hardest for those of us in ministry. We can be so busy doing work *for* Jesus—preparing the slides for worship, changing the roll of check-in printer labels, restocking the crayons—that we forget to slow down and simply be present *with* Jesus and his people.

Jesus targeted his teaching about humility toward those who thought highly of themselves and wished to be great.[15] He insisted that these disciples think of themselves less and think more of the lowly, the little ones. But within the span of a chapter, his ambitious trainees forgot his lessons about humility and the value of children. Before long, the disciples were rebuking the people for bringing children near (Matt. 19:13). It's one of only a few places in the Gospels where Jesus becomes angry (Mark 10:14; see also Mark 3:5; John 2:13–16). Excluding children from Christ's presence is serious business. But leadership seasoned with the gospel does the opposite. The gospel helps us see our own neediness, and at the same time, reminds us that we have been welcomed by the Savior. He has not despised us. So, in light of his welcome, we can extend hospitality to others. We can even welcome children in Jesus's name.

When leaders in a local church, those regarded as the greatest, begin to embody welcoming love for the little ones—not just for children, but the difficult children for instance with behavioral struggles or disabilities—then it can change a church culture. One Easter Sunday, the two pastors who led our local church's counseling and mercy ministries at the time volunteered to serve in children's ministry for a day. It demonstrated to our volunteer team, families, and our kids just how much our pastoral leadership values the next generation. It was awkward for those guys to do hand motions during the music or manage a classroom; children's ministry is really different from the counseling chair. But our volunteers and families talked about that day for years.

Jesus tells us that leaders in his kingdom demonstrate their greatness when they stoop low to welcome kids. How about you? Will you hear these words, then turn around and just as quickly forget? Don't miss the blessing at the church's front door. Remember, our Savior says, "Whoever receives one such child in my name receives me" (Matt. 18:5).

4

Safety and Security in a Corrupted World

Our Responsibility to Protect
Kids from Abuse

ON SATURDAY NIGHT, November 6, 2011, I went to bed late. I'd stayed up to watch what I thought at the time would be the biggest college football event of the season, an epic matchup between number-one-ranked Louisiana State University and number-two Alabama. The match between the two powerhouses was a defensive slog that ended in a 9–6 overtime victory for LSU. However, in the days that followed, the so-called "Game of the Century"—and every other national college football storyline—was muted by a tragic story.

By the following Wednesday evening, the career of one of the winningest coaches in college football history, Penn State's Joe Paterno, was brought to an end because of a sin of omission. He was fired for his silence.

In 2002, Mike McQueary, a graduate assistant, observed one of Penn State's assistant coaches, defensive coordinator Jerry Sandusky, forcing a young boy into a sexual act in the showers of the school's football locker room. McQueary reported the incident to Paterno, who passed at least some of the details along to two administrators, the school's athletic director and a vice president. No one reported the incident to the police. Sandusky, at the time, ran a non-profit organization for underprivileged boys. He brought the boys onto the Penn State campus when he was a coach; he continued to do so even after his own retirement from the coaching staff; and he continued to do so after the report reached university officials.[1]

Sandusky's actions and Penn State's neglect finally came into public view on that Saturday before Paterno's firing. Sandusky was arrested and charged with forty felony counts of sexual abuse involving at least eight young boys over the span of fifteen years. The two administrators were also arrested and charged with failure to report the abuse and with perjury. The Pennsylvania grand jury also confirmed that both Paterno and Penn State President Graham Spanier had knowledge of the 2002 report of abuse and never contacted the police. Even though those two men were not under investigation, their firing was inevitable once the facts became known. Both men had credible knowledge that at least one young boy had been sexually abused, and neither did anything effective to stop it.

A Severe Warning for a Severe Problem

In chapter 3, we explored what it looks like for a church to show children gospel-seasoned hospitality. But on the heels of teaching his disciples that "whoever welcomes one child like this in my name welcomes me," Jesus gives the strongest of warnings:

> But whoever causes one of these little ones who believe in me to fall away—it would be better for him if a heavy millstone were hung around his neck and he were drowned in the depths of the sea. Woe to the world because of offenses. For offenses will inevitably come, but woe to that person by whom the offense comes. If your hand or your foot causes you to fall away, cut it off and throw it away. It is better for you to enter life maimed or lame than to have two hands or two feet and be thrown into the eternal fire. And if your eye causes you to fall away, gouge it out and throw it away. It is better for you to enter life with one eye than to have two eyes and be thrown into hellfire. (Matt. 18:6–9 CSB)

The picture Jesus paints with his warning is graphic and severe. He tells his disciples that drowning at sea with a heavy grindstone—literally a made-for-a-donkey millstone—fastened around one's neck is *better* than the eternal fate in hellfire that awaits those who cause one of the little ones who believe in him to fall away. The warning is also broad. Jesus addresses *any person* who would cause a little one to "stumble" (NIV), "sin" (ESV), or "fall away" (CSB). He's strongly cautioning *anyone* who might cause someone young in their belief to falter and leave the faith behind.[2]

What are the sinful offenses Jesus is confronting? In the immediate context, the Savior's words are directed to those who have an inflated sense of self-importance (Matt. 18:1–4). Arrogance can tempt people to disregard kids or lead others to stand between children and Jesus (19:13–15). But in addition to confronting their pride, Jesus also instructs his disciples to deal harshly with their hands, feet, and eyes if these parts of the body become a cause for offense (18:8–9). He used the same hyperbolic imagery in his Sermon on the Mount (5:29–30). In that passage, Jesus was confronting anger and sexual lust (5:21–28).

In the strongest of terms, Jesus warns against the pride, lust, and anger that is at work in the hearts of those who sexually molest and physically harm children. He tells his disciples that such sin can damage a child's faith. The first representation a child has of God is their parents and regular caregivers.[3] So when children see or experience abuse at the hands of the people who should be the most nurturing, it can impede their capacity for trust.[4] This reality should sober us and encourage us to be vigilant about protecting kids.

Coming to Terms with Our Own Corruptibility

It's hard to describe the ripple effect that the Penn State scandal had on college football. Joe Paterno's program was one of the most respected in the country. But the Sandusky scandal exposed the hard truth that depravity and sin reach even to places that look squeaky clean. As Michael Weinreb, a sports reporter and Penn State alumnus who grew up near the university, wrote for the sports blog *Grantland*, "We've come to terms with the corruptibility of the human soul in State College, and we've swept away the naïve notion that this place where we lived so quietly was different from the rest of America."[5]

The kind of offenses that cause little ones to stumble are inevitable in a fallen world. Jesus knew this, and he pronounced a woe upon the world because of such offenses (Matt. 18:7).[6] But don't let the fact that Jesus says, "Woe to the world" confuse you. Jesus didn't think that only those outside the faith would be stumbling blocks for children. In verses 8–9, Jesus says, "If *your* hand or *your* foot causes *you* to sin." As Carson observes, "Jesus now abandons denunciation of the world . . . and tells his disciples they may prove to be not only victims but aggressors."[7] Jesus knew that sins which prove to be stumbling blocks to little ones are not merely *out there* in the world, but we find them *in here*, in the church as well.

In recent years, social-media feeds and newspaper headlines have been filled with stories of spiritual leaders—priests, pastors, youth pastors, and volunteers—who are accused of having sent sexually explicit text messages to youth, molesting children, and even raping minors in their care.[8] The trouble isn't limited to one denominational group or one region of the country. Abuse of positions of power to take advantage of children is a problem that affects Catholics and Protestants, mainline churches and evangelicals, from the coast of Florida to the Puget Sound.

Some will suggest that the news stories are simply schemes to slander Christians' reputations, but given Christ's warnings in Matthew 18:6–9, we shouldn't dismiss them so quickly. While it wouldn't be appropriate for us to join an ungodly culture and "pile on" fellow believers, I am prayerful that the onslaught of reports will wake up church leaders and lead them to take policy violations and reports of sexual misconduct seriously. It's important that we come to terms with our own corruptibility. It's important that we see that abuses not only happen in the locker rooms of secular universities, but that they may also be happening in our own ministries, at the hands of people we trust.

How Can We Miss Something So Monstrous?

It's hard to believe that the Penn State administration or a group of God-loving elders at a local church could allow abuse to continue undetected under its collective nose. But it's easier to fall asleep at the wheel than you might think. I can't speak to the motives at play in every situation, but I can speak to two everyday temptations that can keep Christian leaders from responding to suspected or reported abuse appropriately.

First, we make false assumptions about what a sexual predator is like. Penn State's Jerry Sandusky was one of those people folks didn't see coming. In 1977, Sandusky had started a recreational program for troubled boys. Over time, that program had turned into a respected statewide charity. Sandusky would host neighborhood softball games and was known for being a cutup who would orchestrate regular water-balloon fights with the kids in his care.[9] He was the last person people would have pegged as a sexual predator. But, as Deepak Reju observes, Sandusky's life lines up with one of the typical profiles:

> He's *not* disheveled and disliked. He *is* someone who is respected and highly revered in his community. He's *not* someone who is poor and socially isolated. He *is* someone who has influence and money. He is *not* someone who abducted a child and forced him to do lewd things. He *is* someone who regularly spent time with troubled children and lavished gifts and special treatment on them. He is *not* someone suspected of being abusive to

young children. He *is* someone who was thought to be doing great good for kids through his charity work and adoption of six children.[10]

Sandusky wasn't a *power predator*, the kind that takes a child by sheer force—like a bear stealing food from a campsite. He was a *persuasion predator*. Like a circling shark, this type of abuser uses "personality, charm, and influence to convince others that he is trustworthy," only to strike when the moment is right.[11]

Child molesters are seductive. They typically demonstrate strong interpersonal skills with children, and they will cultivate a relationship with them over a long period of time, often grooming a child with attention and gifts. Sandusky would take children to football games and invite them for sleepovers in his home. Persuasion predators like him work hard to be liked and respected. They're counting on making the sort of impression that will make any suspicions about their true behavior seem unbelievable.[12]

If Sandusky had looked disheveled, been economically poor, or had known psychiatric problems, Mike McQueary and the Penn State officials probably wouldn't have thought twice before alerting the authorities. But when faced with suspicion about someone they respected—someone they liked, one of their own—they gave a serial abuser the benefit of the doubt.[13]

Are we any different? The truth is that many Christians default to the most innocent explanation. After all, in most situations, assuming the best is a polite way of maintaining civility and friendship. Moreover, when someone reports abuse about someone we know, love, and respect, we'll typically bristle, wanting to deny it and defend the accused.[14] This is why it's essential that children's ministries have universally applied protocols for protection and reporting. At critical moments, we need policies and procedures that will guard us against the danger of our own false assumptions.

Second, we fail to see the way that our role influences the way we interpret each situation. As Christians, we believe that God often assigns people with varying gifts and complementary roles so they can work together to address complex tasks. In the care of a local church, God assigned differing roles to pastors and deacons (1 Tim. 3:1–13). He's assigned differing gifts and roles to each of the church's members "for building up the body of Christ, until we all attain to the unity of the faith and of the knowledge of the Son of God" (Eph. 4:11–13; cf. Rom. 12:3–8). When it comes to addressing severe sin, God has assigned church leadership and the governing authorities differing but complementary roles as well (Matt. 18:15–20; Rom. 13:1–7).

Our differing gifts and roles influence the way we assess and respond to severe sin. Brad Hambrick, a pastor and biblical counselor, describes this phenomenon with what he calls a "parable of blades." He writes,

> When you hand a surgeon a blade, they think "scalpel." When you hand a fisherman a blade, they think "filet." When you hand a chef a blade, they think "julienne." While the shape of the knife should make it obvious what it is for, you get the point—the role of a person impacts how he or she interprets a situation.[15]

As Christian leaders, we have a redemptive mission. We want to see new spiritual life flourish as we proclaim Christ's message of grace, reconciliation, and forgiveness. When we hear the word "abuse," we tend to think of it as a strong moral category rather than as a legal category. We use phrases like "severe sin," not "crime." If we're honest, policies and legal requirements put us off. Such strictures aren't life giving, because they have a restrictive, not a restorative, purpose. When ministers think about how to address severe sin, it's typical for us to turn to biblical passages on church discipline like Matthew 18:15–20.[16] This passage, after all, follows closely after the Matthew 18:6–9 warning I unpacked at the beginning of this chapter. The goal of such passages is to confront sin, call for repentance, and restore the sinner to fellowship (Matt. 18:15; cf. 2 Cor. 2:5–10; Gal. 6:1; James 5:19–20).

But if a call to repentance—not a call to Child Protective Services—is our first impulse in the case of abuse, our perspective has become myopic. Our view has been shaped by our redemptive ministry role, and we've failed to take into account the responsibility God also has given to government. Policies, procedures, and laws are necessary. God has given them to us for the purpose of exposing sin and restraining evil ("[the ruler] does not bear the sword in vain," Rom. 13:4). We can't ignore them. We must remember that reporting abuse and neglect is mandated when it is against a minor.[17] Neither fear of making a false accusation nor an arrogant thought that the church can do a better job investigating the incident than the authorities should lead us to disobey the law and thus endanger the children in our care. As R. Albert Mohler Jr. wrote immediately following the Penn State arrests, "Waiting for further information allows a predator to continue and puts children at risk."[18]

WHAT DO WE DO WHEN WE HAVE BOTH LEGAL AND PASTORAL RESPONSIBILITIES?[19]

1. If civil authorities need to be involved, make sure they are notified. In the case of suspected child abuse or neglect, you are a mandatory reporter. You do not need to conduct an investigation to justify your suspicions. You are simply required to report.

2. View civil authorities as complementary teammates who have the same initial objective: the safety of the child. The jurisdictional authority of a social worker or police officer can help promote safety in a way that a pastor, deacon, or small group leader cannot. We should be grateful for their involvement.

3. Realize the legal process may delay some aspects of ministry involvement. Church leaders can be frustrated when a social worker asks them not to talk to a child's parents, when an attorney advises silence about allegations until after a trial, when waiting on a series of hearings, or when a restraining order interferes with communication. However, these delays are not a reason to begin to view the civil authorities as a competitor in your pastoral care efforts.

4. Seek to be an asset to the civil authorities. When church leaders fulfill their role in notifying the civil authorities, civil authorities are more prone to view church leaders as an asset to their work. In your interactions with Child Protective Services, the police, or a social worker, ask the question, "How can we help?"

**5. Realize that even though the church's role is broader (redemptive) and longer (not just to the resolution of the legal concern), the input and expertise of the civil authorities can be very helpful to good pastoral care. How civil authorities gauge the severity of an abuse case can be a helpful reference point for a church. Churches do not have the same level of day-to-day experience with criminal acts compared to law enforcement, so we should seek to learn from their wisdom as we deal with abusers and victims.

Creating a Child Protection Policy

What happened at Penn State is a terrible tragedy, but even if you've taken steps to question your own assumptions about both child predators and the governing authorities, what is to keep abuse from happening in your ministry? Many churches create a child protection policy in order to describe the parameters of a safe environment before a problem arises. Reju writes, "A child protection policy (CPP) is a set of self-imposed guidelines that describes how a church intends to protect and care for the children under its care."[20]

I want to walk through what it might look like for your local church to put a CPP in place for the first time. The following six steps are also helpful if you have a CPP. They'll help you to ensure that your policies are protecting the kids in your care in the way that they should.

First, put together a team. This should be a multi-disciplinary group of individuals who will be responsible to develop and implement the child protection policy. They'll serve as the team putting the policy in place, and they may continue after its adoption as a committee that ensures ongoing compliance and/or certification.

Include your children's and student ministry staff, the pastoral team giving oversight to this process, key volunteers, and anyone else in your church community who could give insight (e.g., social workers, counselors, lawyers, police officers, or child advocates). You may have educators in your church who have been trained in creating emergency response plans or following active-shooter protocols, and they can bring their experience to bear for your local church. At the church where I served for many years, one of our elders' wives worked as a social worker for women who had been sexually assaulted. Her experience was vital for our team as we developed care plans.

Second, do your homework. At the end of part 2 of this book, I've listed a number of written resources on children's ministry safety and security. Be sure to consult them. The first book I'd encourage you to read on child safety is Reju's *On Guard: Preventing and Responding to Child Abuse at Church.* His book will help you identify all of the big child protection categories: governance and church polity, screening and background checks, children's ministry check-in and check-out processes, facility design, training, as well as how to put together a response plan. Once these key categories are identified (compare the ECAP standards in chart 4.1), it may be helpful for your team to embrace a divide-and-conquer approach. Assign a team member to research each key protection policy category and then to report back to the team as a whole for discussion.

Third, seek out outside experts. Your team might consider seeking out an outside group like Church Law & Tax (churchlawandtax.com), the Evangelical Council for Abuse Prevention (ECAP, ecap.net), GRACE: Godly Response to Abuse in the Christian Environment (netgrace.org), or Ministry Safe (ministrysafe.com). Some of these groups have resources and people who can help you to craft a customized child protection policy for your church. Some offer certification or even accreditation programs that include on-site property inspections for churches and ministries. Each of the groups has its own emphasis, and they each have different offerings.

- *Church Law & Tax* is one of the best places to find out about new legal developments in your state.
- *ECAP* is sponsored by and works closely with local churches, legal experts, victim advocates, and church insurance companies. They've worked hard to develop abuse prevention standards for the accreditation of evangelical churches and ministries.
- *GRACE* focuses on local church training and victim advocacy; their goal is to empower Christian communities to recognize, prevent, and respond to abuse.
- *Ministry Safe* is a background check company. They will help you put a protection plan and training process together, but their core competency is doing background checks and volunteer vetting.

Fourth, adopt policies and procedures. Don't research forever. It's essential to put your policies down on paper. When you get to the writing stage, be sure to look at Basyle Tchividjian and Shira Berkovits's *The Child Safeguarding Policy Guide* as well as Jack Crabtree's *Better Safe Than Sued.* By providing concrete examples, these books will help you craft clear written policies and procedures. They'll show you language that other churches have chosen to use in their CPP as well as in their volunteer applications, liability release forms, and reporting forms. Crabtree's book focuses on protecting students in youth ministry. It can help you answer questions like, "How do I vet church van drivers who help us take students to camp? What first aid training is helpful or necessary for winter or water sports? If we take kids on an overnight trip, what kind of liability forms do we need?" ECAP's standards (chart 4.1) and your church insurance company are also helpful resources when creating policies and procedures.

Fifth, begin training and implementation. As you approach this stage, remember that while your committee may have spent months thinking about the new policies, other staff and volunteers will probably hear about new policies for the first time when they come to training. You must keep this in mind so that you train at a pace that allows your team to digest new policies, understand the reasoning behind them, and learn them well. One of the best resources I'm aware of to help you to train your team is the free *Becoming a Church That Cares Well for the Abused* videos and handbook (churchcares.com). The contributors to this training will walk your staff and volunteers through key responses to physical and sexual abuse as well as through what happens when a reporting call is placed to Child Protective Services.

Finally, review your CPP at least annually. You'll want to review any reports to CPS that have been made, any known policy violations, or any other issues that arise. Churches should keep clear records of these matters and the parties involved. This is not a naughty list (so that you can give particular volunteers smaller coffee mugs at Christmas.) No, you write down anything that might help you to adapt your training plan or make necessary adjustments to your CPP.

Chart 4.1

ECAP Member Standards for Child Protection

The Evangelical Council for Abuse Prevention (ECAP) lists child protection standards that are expected of their accredited members under the following five major categories:

---

1. Governance:
"Organizations shall provide effective governance and have clear and effective documents concerning the structure, operations, and beliefs of the organization that are consistent with child safety."

This standard covers matters of church polity and theological integrity, including the adoption of a theological statement on gender identity. ECAP's accredited members must purchase liability insurance, keep appropriate records on all personnel, and adopt an annually reviewed child protection plan with clear policies on matters such as personnel/child ratios, appropriate touch, and check-in and check-out procedures.

---

2. Child Safety Operations:
"Organizations shall have clear and effective written policies in place to guide staff and volunteers for both day-to-day operations, for all off-site activities, and for specific care as it relates to small children. Organizations shall prioritize transparency, including guidelines for visibility in public areas related to work with minors."

In addition to requiring written policies and procedures, this standard seeks to ensure that ministry facilities for childcare maintain enough visibility for safety and security. ECAP expects member organizations to have policies in place for any and all off-site events.

---

3. Screening:
"Organizations shall develop and implement a detailed screening process for employees and volunteers that includes a written application, waiting period, personal interview (or other sufficient personal interaction), reference checks, and a background check from a reputable provider. If at any point in the screening process prior unlawful or immoral activity is uncovered, the organization shall deal with the applicant based on clearly defined thresholds for disqualification."

The ECAP standards indicate the kinds of questions and requirements that are important for application, background check, and screening processes as well as the type of background check that should be run on each applicant.

---

4. Training:

"Organizations shall provide training for all employees and volunteers who work with children, as well as bystanders in the general ministry setting. The training shall comply with state laws, regulations, and minimum requirements, as well as offer guidelines for reporting and responding to child safety violations. Employees and volunteers who work directly with minors shall be trained on appropriate limits and controls for any contact with minors outside of ministry activities."

ECAP outlines standards for first-time and refresher training that covers abuse indicators as well as reporting processes.

5. Response:

"Organizations shall have written policies and procedures, including a full incident response plan, which shall outline the proper methods and timing for reporting abuse allegations to all those who should have knowledge of an incident."

ECAP expects accredited members to have written response plans that include notifications and reports to all appropriate parties including Child Protective Services and a communication plan for all organization members and stakeholders. They also outline standards for follow-up investigations of the organization itself after an incident.

See detailed versions of these standards and the recommendations attached to each at the ECAP website (ecap.net).

Here's an example of why adjustments are necessary: I served as a local church children's minister for fifteen years. When I began in ministry, smartphones were not what they are today. Now every teacher comes to class with a camera in their phone. One day, two of our college student volunteers photographed their class and posted the picture on Instagram. This concerned two parents, so we addressed it personally with the two college students, encouraging them that—as a matter of wisdom—they shouldn't post photos of other people's children on social media. But later, when reviewing our training, one of our staff members pointed out that a number of kids in our care were in the foster system. She observed that posting a picture of one of these kids online might violate our state's standards for foster families. So we made it a policy—and a regular part of our training—to never take pictures of kids during class and post them on the web. That's just one example. Here's the bottom line: think of your CPP as an evolving tool that can change and improve as your ministry circumstances demand.

Watch Your Church. Watch Yourself.

Putting a child protection policy and plan like this in place is essential, because Christians have a fundamental responsibility to protect vulnerable children. Reju writes, "We learn this sense of protection from God who throughout the Bible has a special burden for the young, weak, and oppressed in society."[21] Jesus's strong warning teaches us to beware the corruption of this fallen world but also to beware the corruption of our own fallen hearts.

To welcome kids into gospel-seasoned environments, we need more than a warm welcome; we also need vigilance. We must be vigilant about rooting out false assumptions, properly vetting volunteers, and implementing our protection plans. We don't do this in a legalistic spirit, thinking that policies will bring life. No, our vigilance is rooted in humility and self-awareness. Who among us has not seen anger and lust in their own heart? The last thing we want is to allow unchecked sin to become a gospel-preventing stumbling block for the next generation.

We're vigilant, because in rooting out stumbling blocks, we're cultivating the kind of children's ministry environments where seeds of faith can take root and grow.

Reflection on Part 2

Create Welcoming Environments

TAKE A LOOK at the activities and questions for reflection and evaluation below. Before you move on, spend some time working through them and thinking about your ministry's safety and hospitality.

Questions for Reflection and Evaluation

1. Read Hebrews 10:19–25 again. List out all of the things that Christ has done to welcome you into his presence. Do you regularly experience the confidence this passage describes when coming before the Lord in prayer? Do you experience this confidence when moving toward his people? Meditating on the truths described here can give you confidence. Which of the realities that you listed do you find the most encouraging?

2. We show Jesus to kids through the way we practice hospitality. We want ministries that are kid-friendly and welcoming. Evaluate your ministry's hospitality based on the following four categories. For each area, give yourself a ranking from 1 to 5.

✮ ✮ ✮

Humble and God-Dependent   1   2   3   4   5

Is your ministry seasoned with grace-filled humility? Do you have a time of regular prayer that sets the atmosphere for your time together? Is your team ready to respond with warmth to a family or child that is not typical for your ministry—a child with a disability or special needs, a family that does not speak English as their first language, or a family with a different ethnic background from the majority in your community?

Child-Targeted   1   2   3   4   5

Do your ministry environments have a kid-friendly and bright atmosphere? Do kids enjoy their time in your children's ministry classes? Would they be eager to invite their lost friends?

A Warm Welcome   1   2   3   4   5

Do you have team members who are trained to engage new families at check-in? Are these team members clearly identifiable with nametags, lanyards, or t-shirts? Does your facility have adequate signage? Is the technology that you use for check-in up to date and user friendly? Have you observed hospitality volunteers lingering in conversation with new families? Do you follow up with new families by sending thank-you notes or care packages?

Valuing Kids as Part of the Community   1   2   3   4   5

Do your children's ministry teachers know regular kids by name? Are church leaders mindful of the next generation as they plan worship services and other events? Are there opportunities for youngsters to serve side-by-side with adults?

✩ ✩ ✩

After you've ranked your ministry in all four areas, chose the two areas that scored the lowest. Is there one new practice you could adopt to help your ministry to grow in this area?

3. How would your leadership team respond to allegations of child abuse against a church leader? Be honest. Would leaders try to minimize the accusation—caring more about your church's reputation than about protecting vulnerable children? Would you consider handling charges internally instead of reporting possible abuse to the appropriate authorities? What safeguards might you put in place now to avoid these failures?[1]

4. Does your church have a child protection plan (CPP)? If not, begin working through the steps outlined in chapter 4 to create one. If you do have a CPP, consider if you are weak in one of the five ECAP standard areas (chart 4.1). If so, how can you improve?

For Further Study

On Creating Welcoming Environments

Miller, Sue, and David Staal. *Making Your Children's Ministry the Best Hour of Every Kid's Week.* Grand Rapids, MI: Zondervan, 2004.

Ward, Virgina, Reggie Joiner, and Kristen Ivy. *It's Personal: Five Questions You Should Answer to Give Every Kid Hope.* Cumming, GA: reThink Group, 2019.

On Church Safety and Security

Crabtree, Jack. *Better Safe Than Sued: Keeping Your Students and Ministry Alive.* Grand Rapids, MI: Zondervan/Youth Specialties, 2009.

Hambrick, Brad, ed. *Becoming a Church That Cares Well for the Abused Handbook.* Nashville, TN: B&H Publishing, 2019.

Reju, Deepak. *On Guard: Preventing and Responding to Child Abuse at Church.* Greensboro, NC: New Growth Press, 2014.

Tchividjian, Basyle, and Shira M. Berkovits. *The Child Safeguarding Policy Guide for Churches and Ministries.* Greensboro, NC: New Growth Press, 2017.

PART 3

CONNECT KIDS
TO CHRIST

5

Three Ways to Tell a Bible Story

The Priority of Gospel-Centered Teaching

ONE OF MY RESPONSIBILITIES when I served as a pastor over children's ministry was to observe our volunteer team as they taught kids each week. I liked to peek into the classrooms and hang out with the kids while they were eating Goldfish crackers. One week, I observed a class learning about Israel crossing the Red Sea. I sat down with the kids during their snack, and I asked, "Who was your story about today?"

One child answered, "We learned about God!"

I dismissed that as a typical Sunday school answer, and I followed up, "Yes, but didn't you learn about Moses? What did Moses do?"

The kid was brilliant. "Moses didn't do much," he said. "He just prayed and lifted his stick. But God dried up the sea so the people could cross. Then, God drowned all the Egyptians! God was awesome!" That kid got the lesson's point better than I did.

It's easy to miss the point when we're teaching kids. Many children's Bible resources are written to teach children what to do: *Be joyful! Be courageous!* But this is rarely the main point of a Bible story. God gave us Scripture to reveal himself and his plan of salvation for us through his Son, Jesus Christ.

As teachers, we have an incredible responsibility. The Bible tells us that we incur a stricter judgment (James 3:1). God has entrusted the next generation into our hands. But what will the kids in our classrooms remember after we've finished teaching? What characters in the story will they most want to identify with and be like? How will they grow in their understanding of God and the gospel?

Let's walk through three different ways you could teach a Bible story.

Approach #1: The Example Lesson

The most natural place for children's ministry teachers to begin is to look at a Bible story and think about what models should be followed—or avoided. This is the *example lesson*. This is a perfectly legitimate way to think about the Bible text. In 1 Corinthians 10, Paul recounts the story of Israel's journey through the wilderness. He tells how the Israelites were given the benefits of salvation through the sea and how God provided spiritual food for them and water from the rock (vv. 1–4). Nevertheless, a whole generation died in the wilderness due to God's judgment on their idolatry and grumbling (vv. 5–10). Paul warns the Corinthians they may also incur God's judgment if they revert to setting their hearts on evil things (v. 6). He writes, "Now these things happened to them [the Israelites] *as an example*, but they were written down for our instruction, on whom the end of the ages has come" (v. 11).

If Paul was content to use an example lesson, we can too! With an example lesson, kids will identify with the hero or villain, and they'll learn examples to follow or avoid. You've probably heard the story of David and Goliath taught in this way. According to this method, the point of the story is to be brave and face big obstacles with courage. Or—in the world of *Veggie Tales*—"little guys can do big things too!"[1]

When we tell the story this way, kids remember key characters and little details. They may remember how David carried ten loaves of bread to his brothers and ten cheeses to the commander of their unit (1 Sam. 17:17–18)—just the perfect ingredients for making ten pizzas! They'll remember how David was too little for Saul's armor (vv. 38–39), how he took five smooth stones and a sling (v. 40), and that he cut off Goliath's head (v. 51). The kids will also remember to be brave like David, because David is the example to follow.

That's one way to tell the story. An example lesson makes clear what God wants us to do and what we shouldn't do. But if we just teach example lessons, what will kids learn about God?

Approach #2: The God-Centered (or Theologically Driven) Lesson

A *God-centered* or *theologically driven lesson* helps kids to focus on God as the main character of each Bible story. This approach is grounded in the conviction that the Bible was written to show us who God is and what he's done for us. Therefore, one of the first things we should ask ourselves when preparing a Bible lesson is this: What is *God* doing in this story?[2]

When we're teaching 1 Samuel 17, we shouldn't forget about David, but that shouldn't keep us from seeing that God is the true hero in this story. In fact, do you remember what David said to king Saul? "*The LORD* that delivered me out of the paw of the lion, and out of the paw of the bear, *he* will deliver me out of the hand of this Philistine" (v. 37 KJV). When Goliath came against him with a sword and spear and javelin, David didn't start naming his weapons: "Well, here I come with my sling!" No way! David said, "I come against you *in the name of the LORD Almighty, the God of the armies of Israel*, whom you have defied" (v. 45 NIV). David knows that the battle belongs to the Lord. If we're listening to David's words, we begin to understand that this story gives us more than David's example. It's a story about *God* and the salvation he brings.

Teaching God-centered lessons is a vast improvement over only teaching example lessons. But I think teaching only God-centered lessons doesn't quite go far enough either. All of us know kids—and adults for that matter—who know the truth with their heads but who haven't had it affect their hearts. I want to suggest an approach that moves beyond theological knowledge to grace-motivated, personal change.

Approach #3: The Gospel-Centered Lesson

The final way to tell a Bible story is the *gospel-centered lesson*. The apostle Paul makes clear that the gospel message alone is enough for Christian growth. In all his letters, Paul emphasizes that God's appointed Savior, his Son Jesus Christ, is the main character of the Bible.

But, sadly, it's possible to teach the Bible without ever talking about Jesus. To the religious leaders in his day, Jesus said, "You

GOSPEL-CENTERED TEACHING

Gospel-centered teaching requires both understanding a Bible text in its original context and then relating the plot of that story to the Bible's larger Christ-centered storyline.

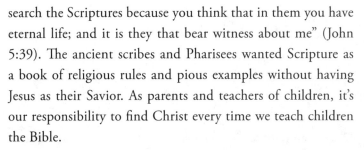

search the Scriptures because you think that in them you have eternal life; and it is they that bear witness about me" (John 5:39). The ancient scribes and Pharisees wanted Scripture as a book of religious rules and pious examples without having Jesus as their Savior. As parents and teachers of children, it's our responsibility to find Christ every time we teach children the Bible.

In his book *Preaching Christ from the Old Testament*, Sidney Greidanus defines the gospel-centered approach as teaching lessons that "authentically integrate the message of the text with the climax of God's revelation in the person, work, and/or teaching of Jesus Christ as revealed in the New Testament."[3] Greidanus's approach assumes two interpretational moves. First, we must understand the purpose for which the original human author told this story to his audience. Second, we need to relate the plot of this story to the Bible's larger storyline.[4]

How do we go about that task?

I once had a conversation with pastor Marty Machowski and some other children's ministry leaders about the best ways to craft a gospel-centered lesson. He told us, "We want to understand who in this Bible story needs the good news.

Then, we want to help our kids relate to them." To craft a gospel-centered lesson, we should first help kids identify with the neediest people in the passage, those who are desperate for salvation. We should ask, "Who in this story *needs* the good news?"

In the David and Goliath story, the people who need salvation the most are the Israelites. They have a strong enemy, Goliath, and a weak leader, King Saul. When Goliath marches out into the valley of Elah to challenge the king, he challenges all of Israel as well as Israel's God. In that moment, Israel needed a courageous hero to save them. Saul should have been the first soldier on the battlefield to confront Goliath, but he was puny and paralyzed. As a result, his army was paralyzed too.

What does God do to help Israel in their great need?

God sends David. The people there didn't know it yet, but we know that David stepped onto that battlefield as Israel's newly anointed king (1 Samuel 16). The shepherd boy from Bethlehem was the people's representative. When God won the battle for the people, he won the battle *through* David.

Now that we've discovered what God is doing for his needy people in the story, we should relate this passage to the Bible's larger storyline. In other words, we should look for how God's action in this little plotline points to what Jesus has done for us in the Bible's larger story. Jack Klumpenhower has phrased the key question this way: How does God do the same for us—only better—in Jesus?[5]

When you ask this question, you may start to see that David points beyond himself. The boy-savior gives us a sneak peek into a specific way God rescues his people: God saves his people by sending them a representative king, a child from Bethlehem who crushes the head of his enemy. Sound familiar? David is the hero, but David points to Jesus.

By first helping kids identify with the people in the story who need the good news and then looking for the ways God brings good news to these needy people, we discover specific ways Jesus wants to bring good news to *us*. We discover the particular ways believing the gospel will give us life and hope.

The message of 1 Samuel 17 is good news for us, because, like David, we do fight giants. The kids we teach live in a world of skeptics who speak against our faith. The temptation is to look at the world and believe that what you see is what you get. Christians often have less power and less money, and we may not be as successful as worldly giants; why keep living a godly life and standing against temptation? We can be frozen in insecurity and fear. But we don't have to be, because there is a boy from Bethlehem who has already cut off the head of our enemy. Knowing Jesus fought for them gives kids confidence. This kind of gospel-centered lesson not only teaches kids how Christ is the central figure of the Bible, but also, in seeing him, they'll find deep and powerful motivation, the kind which will help them change the way they live.

Putting Gospel-Centered Interpretation into Practice

I believe we should be aiming for gospel-centered lessons. But you can have gospel-centeredness as an ideal and still struggle with how to make your lesson center around Jesus. I've found the following grid (See chart 5.1) to be a helpful tool for my own teaching preparation.

Chart 5.1

Putting Gospel-Centered Interpretation into Practice

Scripture Passage: I Samuel 17			
What's the purpose of this story in its original context?		How does this particular story relate to the Bible's larger storyline?	
The Need Who in this story needs good news?	**God's Actions** What is God doing for his people in this story?	**Good News!** How does God do the same for us—only better—in Jesus?	**Believe It!** How does believing this good news change the way we live?
Israel, because they had a . . . -strong enemy -weak king	God sent . . . -a new king -a shepherd boy from Bethlehem -someone who represented the people -someone who defeated the enemy	Jesus is . . . -our new King -our Savior from Bethlehem -our representative -the one who will crush Satan's head	We can have confidence to fight sin and temptation even when we feel weak, because we know that Jesus fought Satan for us.

Here's how it works. At the top of the page, I'll write the Scripture address for the passage I'm preparing to teach. Below that, I sketch out four columns. The columns are dedicated to my notes that answer these four questions:[6]

- **The Need.** Who in this story *needs* good news?
- **God's Actions.** What is *God* doing for his people in this story?

- **Good News!** How does God do the same for us—only better—*in Jesus?*
- **Believe It!** How does *believing* this good news change the way we live?

At the end of part 3, I've included some reflection activities which give you the opportunity to try out gospel-centered interpretation for yourself. But before you jump into lesson preparation, let's unpack these four questions a little more. In the next chapter, I'll explain this interpretation method by walking you through another Old Testament story, the story of King Nebuchadnezzar's second dream found in Daniel 4:1–37.

6

The Proud King's Nightmare

Putting Gospel-Centered
Interpretation into Practice

I ONCE TAUGHT through the first half of the book of Daniel during vacation Bible school. As I studied Daniel's opening chapters, I initially expected to learn a lot from the stories' heroes—Daniel, Shadrach, Meshach, and Abednego. But as I prepared these lessons, I kept in mind the teaching preparation questions we discussed in chapter 5. I wrote the Scripture passage, Daniel 4:1–37, at the top of my page, and then I sketched out four columns below with these headings:

- **The Need.** Who in this story *needs* good news?
- **God's Actions.** What is *God* doing for his people in this story?
- **Good News!** How does God do the same for us—only better—*in Jesus*?
- **Believe It!** How does *believing* this good news change the way we live?

I began by thinking about Marty Machowski's counsel: I wanted to help our kids identify with the people in the passage who most needed the good news. What surprised me as I studied was that this was King Nebuchadnezzar; I needed to learn a lot from this proud, idol-worshiping pagan!

Who Needs the Gospel? Proud King Nebuchadnezzar

As I prepared my lesson on Daniel 4, I read the chapters that came before. I saw that Nebuchadnezzar was a powerful man with a short fuse—far from the model of emotional health! In Daniel 2, the king wanted to put his advisors to death just because they couldn't read his mind (vv. 8–9). And it seems the only thing more powerful than Nebuchadnezzar's temper was his pride. In a fantastic dream, God revealed that Nebuchadnezzar's great dominion would not last (vv. 44–45). Ultimately God's forever kingdom would crush Babylon and every other human kingdom. But somehow this powerful message was lost on Nebuchadnezzar. Instead of responding with humility, the king only remembered that he was "the head of gold" (vv. 37–38).

Shortly thereafter, the king set up a ninety-foot-high image for all the people to worship (Dan. 3:1). You probably know what happens next. Three friends—Shadrach, Meshach, and Abednego—refused to bow to Nebuchadnezzar's statue. Enraged, the king heated up his furnace and threw them into the flames. In that moment, King Nebuchadnezzar encountered God. When he looked into the furnace, there was a fourth man in the fire—someone "like a son of the gods" (3:25). The king inspected the three friends and discovered the fire hadn't touched them. They didn't even smell like they'd been sitting around a campfire, much less like they'd been thrown into a barbeque pit!

Clearly influenced by this incredible miracle, King Nebuchadnezzar acknowledged the true God (3:29), but the king was still leading with threats. Nebuchadnezzar announced that anyone who spoke against the three friends would be cut into pieces and have their homes destroyed. Yikes!

See what I wrote in the first column of my interpretation chart (chart 6.1).

What Does God Do? He Sends a Dream and a Prophet

At the beginning of Daniel 4, Nebuchadnezzar issues another decree. The king had a history of threatening the people under his rule (3:6, 29), but this decree stands in stark contrast.[1] King Nebuchadnezzar's words are amazing: "It is my pleasure to tell you about the miraculous signs and wonders that the Most High God has performed for me" (4:2 NIV). What could have changed the proud king's tone?

God's work to change Nebuchadnezzar's heart begins with a second dream. This time, the king saw a giant tree that was inhabited by animals and birds that rested below its foliage and fruit (Dan. 4:11–12). Then, in the midst of the dream, a heavenly messenger came down and declared that the tree would be cut down to its stump (vv. 14–15). And not only would it be cut down, but the tree would be given the mind of an animal and live in the fields (4:16). That's weird, right? Trees don't eat grass! Had the king had one too many Babylonian cocktails before calling it a night?

When he awoke, he skipped his usual threats and sent for Daniel. After hearing the dream, the prophet interpreted it with

Chart 6.1

Our Need: Who in This Story Needs the Gospel?

Scripture Passage: Daniel 4:1-37			
The Need Who in this story needs good news?	God's Actions	Good News!	Believe It!
Nebuchadnezzar because of his . . . - short fuse - coercive threats - idolatry - pride			

trepidation, knowing it portended bad news. He told Nebuchadnezzar that the king himself was the tree (4:22). He'd grown great and strong; his kingdom reached to the ends of the earth. But just as the tree would be cut down, King Nebuchadnezzar would also lose his power and be sent into the wilderness to live and eat like a wild animal. All this would happen because of the king's pride.

It took courage for Daniel to confront the king's sin and speak such a dour message. But the prophet's rebuke was not given without hope. Daniel appealed to the king to turn from his sin before it was too late:

King Nebuchadnezzar, please take my advice. Stop sinning and do what is right. Break from your wicked past and be merciful to the poor. Perhaps then you will continue to prosper. (Dan. 4:27 NLT)

Sadly, Nebuchadnezzar paid little attention to Daniel's warning. One year later, the king walked onto his balcony and began to boast: "Is not this great Babylon, which I have built by my mighty power as the royal residence and for the glory of my majesty?" (Dan. 4:30). Immediately, a voice from heaven announced that the king's power would be removed (vv. 31–32). The king's mind was altered, and he lived like an animal in the fields for seven years. Only then did he come to his senses and say: "Now I, Nebuchadnezzar, praise and exalt and glorify the King of heaven, because everything he does is right and all his ways are just. And those who walk in pride he is able to humble" (v. 37 NIV).

I wrote four key observations in the second column of the interpretation chart. To answer the question, "What is God doing in this story?" I answered:

1. God sent a dream and the prophet Daniel to warn Nebuchadnezzar about his pride.
2. God punished the king when he failed to repent.
3. God restored the king when he humbled himself.
4. God changed the king's threats into a powerful testimony.

Good News! How Does God Do the Same Thing for Us—Only Better—in Jesus?

Our third question for biblical interpretation is: *How does God do the same thing for us—only better—in Jesus?*[2] It's a simple question

Chart 6.2

God's Actions: What Is God Doing in This Story?

Scripture Passage: Daniel 4:1–37			
The Need Who in this story needs good news?	**God's Actions** What is God doing for his people in this story?	Good News!	Believe It!
Nebuchadnezzar because of his . . . – short fuse – coercive threats – idolatry – pride	God sent a dream and the prophet Daniel to warn Nebuchadnezzar about his pride. God punished the king when he failed to repent. God restored the king when he humbled himself. God changed the king's threats into a powerful testimony.		

that has two parts. First, how is what God does for us in Jesus *like* what he did in the story? Second, how is what God does for us in Jesus *better* than what he did in the story?

Let's take the similarities first. As I've unpacked Daniel 4, we've observed how God sent a dream and the prophet Daniel to warn the king about his pride. Daniel risked his life to confront the proud king. *Jesus also put his life on the line for our sin.* That's the first connection I made between Nebuchadnezzar's story and the larger biblical story.

The second connection—how Jesus is better—wasn't quite so clear until I opened some study tools. When I'm preparing to teach from an Old Testament passage, I like to look up the passage in some of my favorite study Bibles. I prefer the notes of *The Reformation Study Bible*, which is free on BibleGateway. com, and the *Biblical Theology Study Bible*.[3] I try to read the notes carefully, and I almost always find that I'm given a cross-reference, which points me to ways this Old Testament passage is referenced in the New. Using the cross-references is a simple method I've used time and again to discover ways the Old Testament passage points forward to Christ. It's like checking my math homework by looking at the answers in the back of the textbook. Here are some examples of connections I've made when using this method (*Hint:* These will help you with the exercises at the end of part 3):

Sometimes I discover *analogies*, New Testament passages which tell me Jesus is *like* someone or something in the Old Testament story. In John 3:14–17, for example, Jesus says he is *like* the bronze serpent Moses lifted up in the wilderness (Num. 21:4–8). How so? When people look to him, they won't perish but instead be saved from death and have eternal life.

Other times, I discover ways Jesus *surpasses* the Old Testament figures. In Matthew 12:42, Jesus says he is *greater than* Solomon. In fact, Jesus goes on to say that the generation which rejected him would be judged, because they should've sought out his wisdom the way the Queen of Sheba sought out Solomon's (1 Kings 10:1–13).

When I looked in my study Bibles at the cross-references in the margin of Daniel 4, I discovered how Jesus is *completely different* from Nebuchadnezzar. Jesus uses the image of the great tree from Nebuchadnezzar's dream in the parable of the mustard seed:

> The kingdom of heaven is like a mustard seed, which a man took and planted in his field. Though it is the smallest of all seeds, yet when it grows, it is the largest of garden plants and becomes a tree, so that the birds come and perch in its branches. (Matt. 13:31–32 NIV)

Jesus not only uses the same tree image in Nebuchadnezzar's dream, he also uses a remarkably similar phrase: that the birds of the air find shelter in the tree's branches (Dan. 4:12; Matt. 13:32). But Jesus describes a kingdom that stands in stark contrast with Nebuchadnezzar's. Babylon grew up with grandeur, but Nebuchadnezzar's kingdom was chopped down because of its pride. The kingdom of heaven by contrast begins with humility, but it grows to be the largest and greatest of all kingdoms.

Now I began to see the big connection between Daniel 4 and Jesus's life. Daniel put his life on the line to confront Nebuchadnezzar's pride. In his humility, Jesus does the same thing for us—but even better! Christ humbled himself, became man, took the form of a servant, and became obedient unto death—even death on a cross (Phil. 2:6–8). In the face of my arrogance, Jesus died to take the punishment my sin deserves. Jesus died for me—even proud me! And because of Jesus's humility, God exalted him and gave him an eternal kingdom:

> Therefore God exalted him to the highest place
>   and gave him the name that is above every name,
> that at the name of Jesus every knee should bow,
>   in heaven and on earth and under the earth,
> and every tongue acknowledge that Jesus Christ is Lord,
>   to the glory of God the Father. (Phil. 2:9–11 NIV)

Now that's a beautiful decree! I wrote the following observations in the third column of the interpretation chart. Jesus is a better king than Nebuchadnezzar because . . .

1. He serves proud sinners in humility.
2. In obedience to the Father, Jesus took the punishment for our pride.
3. Because of his humility, Jesus was exalted and given an eternal kingdom.

How Does Believing This Good News Change the Way I Live?

Nebuchadnezzar shows us that it's better to bow down than to be brought down. As I moved to the final column of the interpretation grid, I felt conviction. The Holy Spirit used this passage to reveal my pride. I often think I'm in charge of my family's faith. I parent pridefully, trusting my methods of discipline or the choices I've made about phone usage and education to ensure my kids will turn out well. When things are going relatively well and I'm posting family vacation pictures on social media, I can be like

Chart 6.3

Good News! How Does God Do the Same Thing for Us—Only Better—in Jesus?

Scripture Passage: Daniel 4:1-37			
The Need Who in this story needs good news?	**God's Actions** What is God doing for his people in this story?	**Good News!** How does God do the same for us—only better—in Jesus?	Believe It!
Nebuchadnezzar because of his . . . - short fuse - coercive threats - idolatry - pride	God sent a dream and the prophet Daniel to warn Nebuchadnezzar about his pride. God punished the king when he failed to repent. God restored the king when he humbled himself. God changed the king's threats into a powerful testimony.	Jesus is a better king than Nebuchadnezzar, because . . . He serves proud sinners in humility. In obedience to the Father, Jesus took the punishment for our pride. Because of his humility, Jesus was exalted and given an eternal kingdom.	

Nebuchadnezzar standing on his balcony and declaring, "Is this not a great family I have built!"

But as I studied Daniel 4, the Spirit brought to mind ways I typically share biblical expectations with my children. Do I win them with the power of threats or with the words of my testimony? Do I coerce them to read their Bibles, or do I model for them what a love for the Scriptures looks like? Am I frustrated with how much time they want to be on screens—spending my time anxiously monitoring them—or do I turn off my own phone and joyfully give them my presence?

Many times, when I'm preparing a lesson for children's ministry, I consider what a faith response will look like for a third grader. It certainly would have been appropriate to talk about ways that kids struggle with pride during this lesson. But as I prepared to teach about King Nebuchadnezzar for our vacation Bible school, I felt God prompting me to be honest about my own sin. Through Daniel 4, I was convicted of the need to confess my pride to my family, and to the kids in our children's ministry as well. I needed to confess my anger and then express joy that I have a great God who gives grace to the humble.

As I wrapped up my time of study, I wrote three observations in the last column of the interpretation chart.

1. Because Christ humbled himself, I can be honest about my anger and pride.
2. I can turn away from anxious pride to joyful humility.
3. I can seek to win others by the power of my testimony.

Keeping Christ Central throughout Your Lesson

In this chapter, I've given you a study method—a set of questions and an interpretation chart—to help you aim for gospel-centered lessons. But even if you've arrived at a Christ-centered interpretation, it can be easy to drift back into old example-lesson habits.

Chart 6.4

Believe It! How Does Believing This Good News Change the Way I Live?

Scripture Passage: Daniel 4:1-37			
The Need Who in this story needs good news?	**God's Actions** What is God doing for his people in this story?	**Good News!** How does God do the same for us—only better—in Jesus?	**Believe It!** How does believing this good news change the way we live?
Nebuchadnezzar because of his . . . - short fuse - coercive threats - idolatry - pride	God sent a dream and the prophet Daniel to warn Nebuchadnezzar about his pride. God punished the king when he failed to repent. God restored the king when he humbled himself. God changed the king's threats into a powerful testimony.	Jesus is a better king than Nebuchadnezzar, because . . . He serves proud sinners in humility. In obedience to the Father, Jesus took the punishment for our pride. Because of his humility, Jesus was exalted and given an eternal kingdom.	Because Christ humbled himself, I can be honest about my anger and pride. I can turn away from anxious pride to joyful humility. I can seek to win others by the power of my testimony.

Pretty soon every class sounds like a lecture: "Don't be proud like King Nebuchadnezzar!"

So how do you keep Jesus central throughout your teaching time? After you fill out that interpretation chart, take a moment to summarize what you've discovered in one *key truth*. Key truths help you keep Jesus front and center in your teaching. Here's how I craft one.

First, I find the key truth provided in our children's ministry curriculum. At the beginning of most children's Bible lessons, you will find a one- or two-sentence summary of the lesson. Sometimes this is called the *story point* or the *big idea*. If your curriculum provides a key truth, locate it.

Second, ensure Jesus is central in this key truth. Some curriculum writers use the key truth merely to summarize the events of the story. For example, the statement for a lesson on Daniel 4 might be something like this: *God used a dream to warn Nebuchadnezzar about his pride.* While that's an accurate summary, it doesn't say enough to help you keep your lesson gospel centered and mission focused.

If you find this is the case with your lesson—or if the curriculum you're using doesn't have a story summary—write one out for yourself. Try to include one "Good News!" truth and one "Believe It!" response from your interpretation chart in your summary. Here is my key truth for the Bible lesson on Daniel 4:

Because Christ humbled himself for us (*good news!*), I can turn away from pride (*believe it!*).

Finally, I put the key truth to memory and repeat it throughout the class time. When I know the lesson truth by heart, I can come back to it again and again and avoid straying from the main point. I use the key truth during the welcome to preview the lesson. I say it again after the story to review what we've just learned. I even review the truth during the craft and while our kids are eating their snack. Sometimes I even have the kids repeat the key truth back to me.

The interpretation chart and the key truth have a purpose. They're tools to help you stay focused on Christ and what he has done (John 5:39; Luke 24:27). Charles Spurgeon describes it this way: "Don't you know . . . that from every town and every village and every hamlet in England, wherever it may be, there is a road to London? So, from every text in Scripture there is a road toward the great metropolis, Christ."[4] Jesus is the capital city of the Bible; every passage contains a road that leads to him. As those commissioned to teach kids, our goal is to find that path and lead children to the great Savior who stands waiting for them at the end.

7

Hands-On, Real-Life, Engaging Discovery

Teaching Kids with Excellence

IMAGINE VISITING a new small group, Bible study, or Sunday school class for the first time. Can you picture in your mind how those gatherings go? First off, there's the introductions. You exchange greetings with at least a few of the other people there—catching up on how Kara's classes are going, the latest with Cedric's grandkids, or Jeff's new job. You might be offered a cup of coffee, and then you'll find a place to sit. After everyone has chatted for a bit, the host or facilitator will begin the meeting—usually by asking for prayer requests. And, once the group has prayed together, you'll begin the lesson. An adult Bible study is typically structured by a lesson outline.

If you're studying through a book of the Bible, the lesson is structured along the lines of the passage's logic or its narrative arc. In most Sunday school classes, you begin by reading a few verses of that week's Scripture passage out loud and then discussing what it means. Any teacher worth their salt will ask you what the "therefore" in verse 1 is there for. Then you'll move deliberately through the text section by section, or even verse by verse. As the meaning of the text becomes clearer, the best teachers will press their group to think about how its meaning relates to everyday life. What are the implications of this passage for Holly's dating relationship or Ivan's business ventures? When the time for study is complete, the facilitator wraps the meeting with prayer and then the participants who gathered begin to take their leave—transitioning from Sunday school to the worship service or home from small group.

Now, think about how different this adult gathering is from a typical children's ministry classroom. Lawrence O. Richards and Gary J. Bredfeldt describe it this way:

> Visit a Sunday school class for two or three year olds and what you'll see probably won't look like teaching. Children will be on the move, playing with blocks or dolls, or looking at colorful books. The room will be large and spacious. . . . [S]tay and listen awhile. Watch the pattern of the activities. Watch the teachers near the activity center. Listen to the simple conversations they have with boys and girls as they play. Stay through the hour and you'll observe a simple Bible story, told clearly and with a variety of visuals. Then more activities—motion songs, finger plays, playing of the story, working at simple paper projects—all of which reinforce the total learning impact. A two year old or three year old class may not look like Sunday school; it may not seem that teaching takes place. Yet in a good department, tots *are* taught.[1]

The differences between an adult class and one for kids is quite striking, isn't it? That's because a room full of toddlers and pre-schoolers is rarely organized around the logic of a Bible passage or even a lesson outline. The lessons are instead structured by the classroom schedule and the environment itself—by a basic routine and activity centers that are designed for play, music, the Bible story, and other games or crafts. In other words, the children's ministry classroom is organized in terms of its *schedule* and its *space*. As each class moves progressively through its routine and the activity centers, all the themes of the Bible story are integrated into all aspects of the lesson environment—into worship, teaching, snacks, and crafts, that is, into the experience of the classroom as a whole.

Learning through Experiences

The truth is that even before children develop the ability to learn cognitively, they are already learning through emotion and experience—through a teacher's facial expressions and example, and through hands-on activities and active games.[2] God knew that kids learn through experience when he made them. That's why when God rescued Israel and gave them his law, he didn't only write it on stone tablets. He communicated through a series of ceremonies that he said would be like "a sign on your hand and as a memorial between your eyes" (Ex. 13:9). Israelite kids *saw* the blood of the Passover sacrifice (12:25–27), *tasted* the unleavened bread (13:6–7), and *sang* about the Lord's great deliverance (15:1). When God did tell the Israelite parents to teach the law and its testimonies in lesson form, he didn't tell them to invite the community's children into a lecture hall. Instead, he said:

And these words that I command you today shall be on your heart. You shall teach them diligently to your children, and shall talk of them when you sit in your house, and when you walk by the way, and when you lie down, and when you rise. You shall bind them as a sign on your hand, and they shall be as frontlets between your eyes. You shall write them on the doorposts of your house and on your gates. (Deut. 6:6–9)

With these words, God instructed the nation's parents to pass along verbal and visual reminders of his commands in various contexts throughout their daily life. We should follow this example today, striving for faithfulness to the biblical message while adopting a flexible teaching approach that emphasizes learning through experience and practice.

This chapter introduces a time-tested teaching method that will help you accomplish that goal. The *Hook, Book, Look, Took (HBLT) method* uses the classroom environment and schedule to cycle through four different ways children learn. In each part of the lesson, you'll organize the truth you're teaching to address specific questions that kids with four different learning styles might ask.[3] Here is the HBLT lesson in outline:

- **Hook—grab their attention!** A Hook activity is designed to introduce and overview the lesson. This is a preparation activity designed to engage the child's senses as well as introduce new vocabulary and concepts. This part of the lesson is intended to capture the attention of the children and to set the stage for God's word. Hook activities speak to the *imaginative learning style*. Kids who are imaginative learners are curious and questioning. They love reflecting on truth and singing or talking about it interpersonally. Imaginative kids learn by listening and sharing their big ideas and feelings. They see the big picture more easily than the small details. So, during the Hook portion of the lesson, it's important to grab the kids' attention, give a broad overview of the lesson's main points, and answer the question, "*Why* do I need to know this?"

- **Book—this is where you school them!** The Book time—sometimes called the "story circle" in a preschool class—is the main focus of the lesson. It's important for teachers to put quality preparation time into studying the Scripture passage and telling clear, interesting, and interactive stories. The truths of the Bible story should be explained in a way the children will understand and enjoy. The Book time speaks to the *analytic learning style*. Analytic learners love facts. These kids expect the teacher to be the primary information giver. They'll sit quietly and listen carefully to all of the information that's presented, and then they'll ask curious questions about the details. To speak to these analytic kids the Book section of a lesson should answer the question, "*What* do I need to know?"

- **Look—make a connection to real life.** In an adult Bible study, the Look time might simply be an application section tacked on at the end. But with kids, it's also important to include creative activities that help children move truth from the Bible to their own hearts and lives. Often, it's helpful to encourage the children to move from the story circle to another location in the teaching area. When children move their bodies, it helps them to transition their thinking. Look activities—which can involve building with blocks, making crafts, and active games—speak to the *pragmatic learning style*. Children who are pragmatic learners enjoy hands-on, active engagement. They love solving problems—so much

Chart 7.1

A Time-Tested, Fourfold Teaching Method

	Reflective	
HOOK		**BOOK**
Imaginative learning style		Analytic learning style
Why do I need to know this?		*What do I need to know?*
Grabs attention		Communicates content and facts
Gives a big picture overview		Tells a clear and interactive story
Introduces new vocabulary/concepts		Uses expression to create interest
Worship / Object Lessons		Video / Visual Aids / "Story Circle"
Abstract		*Concrete*
TOOK		**LOOK**
Dynamic learning style		Pragmatic learning style
What if I put this into practice?		*How does this truth work?*
Inspires creative biblical living		Solves problems
Points back to Christ as motivation		Makes common sense application
Points forward to gospel implications		Connects to real life
Drama / Art		Hands-On Crafts / Active Games
	Active	

so that some pragmatic kids sometimes take things apart just to put them back together. Pragmatic kids play with ideas to make them concrete and workable. So, with the Look portion of our lessons, we're seeking to help kids see that biblical truth is practical and of immediate importance for their lives. We're answering the question, "*How* does this truth work?"

- **Took—motivate dynamic change.** The Took section is similar to the Look section. Both of these parts of the lesson focus on ap-plying biblical truth to a child's life, but the Took *inspires* biblical living by helping kids to imagine the influence following Christ can have on their lives and our world. This section points back to the motivation we find in the gospel, and it points forward to the implications of the gospel. The Took portion of the lesson speaks to the *dynamic learning style*. Like pragmatic kids, dynamic learners enjoy activity as part of the learning process. But rather than looking for practical solutions, dynamic kids excel with creative activities like drama, art, or making music. They see possibilities, intutively move in new directions, thrive when teachers are flexibile, and find real joy in starting a new project on which they can put their unique stamp. During the Took portion of the lesson, it's important to answer the questions, "*What if* I put this truth into practice? What can this become?"

Within each quadrant, students also have preferences for hearing (auditory), seeing (visual), and doing (tactile/kinesthetic). These preferences (or modalities), are sensory channels through which we receive information. Some students in all quadrants are auditory learners. They like listening, singing, clapping, dramatic reading, and hearing music. Others are visual learners. When they see what they are learning through printed words or pictures, they learn better. They love drawing, coloring, photographing, patterns, and forms. Others need to move as part of the learning process. They enjoy methods that involve physical action.[4] As you cycle through the four learning styles, be certain to vary your activities so that they address kids' differing learning modalities as well.

Putting Together a Lesson Plan

The first step toward teaching a great lesson is really studying the Scripture passage, not just the provided lesson materials. It's important for you to dig into the passage. Read it, read the notes in your study Bible or a commentary, and then answer the big questions in the interpretation chart we explored in chapters 5 and 6. A great lesson plan begins with knowing the Scripture passage well.

After I've studied the passage, I'll draw out a four quadrant HBLT grid similar to chart 7.1, and then I'll think through each portion of the chart, writing out activities to use when teaching each portion of the lesson. Here's how I'd think through this process if I were to prepare a lesson on the story about the lame beggar in Acts 3:1–10.

In this passage, a lame man with crippled and crooked legs is carried to the temple daily to beg for charity. One day, as Peter and John went to the temple to pray, the man asked them for money. Peter commanded the man, "Look at us," and then said, "I have no silver and gold, but what I do have I give to you. In the name of Jesus Christ of Nazareth, rise up and walk" (Acts 3:6). Immediately the man's legs became strong and healthy. He leapt up, walked around. He praised God, and the people there joined him.

My observations of this passage led me to summarize it with this key truth: "Because Jesus is better than money, we can trust him to heal our broken world." To see what my interpretation chart for Acts 3:1–10 looked like, see chart 7.2.

Hook—Grab Their Attention!

After studying the Bible passage and filling in the interpretation chart, I work through each part of the lesson. Each lesson begins with one or two Hook activities—songs, action rhymes, or object

Chart 7.2

Interpretation Chart for Acts 3:1–10

Scripture Passage: Acts 3:1-10			
Key Truth: Because Jesus is better than money, we can trust him to heal our broken world.			
The Need Who in this story needs good news?	**God's Actions** What is God doing for his people in this story?	**Good News!** How does God do the same for us—only better—in Jesus?	**Believe It!** How does believing this good news change the way we live?
The man was lame from birth. He had crippled and crooked legs that kept him from work. He was carried to the temple gate every day to beg for charity.	God sent Peter and John to the temple to pray while the man was begging for alms. Peter and John healed the man in Jesus's name. The man's feet and ankles were made strong. The man jumped and walked around, praising Jesus.	Silver and gold could buy the man food and clothes that lasted for a short time, but he'd have to keep coming back to the temple to beg whenever it ran out. Jesus is better than money. Jesus gave complete healing. He changed begging into praise.	Some think our broken world can be fixed if we only have enough money, but money runs out. Instead of trusting wealth, we can trust King Jesus to heal our broken world. We show trust in Jesus by daily praying in his name.

lessons that support the passage's key truth and help the kids see *why* learning this lesson is so important for them right now, at their age, in their relationship with God.

If the curriculum you're using doesn't already have an attention-grabbing Hook or one that clearly answers the *Why* question, you can create one yourself. For our lesson about the crippled beggar, you might bring a pair of crutches to class and then ask the girls and boys to identify them. Ask the children if they've had to use crutches before. Draw the children out and allow them to tell stories about their experiences with broken bones and sprained ankles. Then, answer the *Why* question by saying:

> People use crutches to help them move around when they are hurt. In our world, lots of things break—broken toys, broken hearts, and broken bones. *But Jesus has come to heal our broken world.*

A transition statement like this one at the end of the Hook is an essential way of emphasizing the lesson's key point as you move from each section of the lesson to the next.

Book—This Is Where You School Them!

Telling Bible stories is the heart and soul of children's ministry. Our goal is to help kids see Jesus, and the Bible is where our power and authority for teaching about him comes from (2 Tim. 3:16–17). Many churches have now transitioned from printed Sunday school booklets to digital curriculum. Over the last several years, I've noticed children's ministry teachers at our church telling the Bible story to their class with a phone or an iPad in hand. Using new technology is one way of keeping our notes in front of us, but new tech can also be a distraction. Call me "old school" if you want, but I prefer to put my phone aside when I'm teaching kids. Instead, I pick up a physical copy of God's word—preferably one that's big with a black leather cover and the words "Holy Bible" written in large letters on the binding. Kids are concrete thinkers, and I think it's helpful for them to see that physical representation of how God speaks to us through his book.

Before telling the story, it's good to introduce the lesson by reminding the kids of the authority and importance of Scripture. You might say,

> We are learning from the Bible, God's holy word. We use it the same way hikers use a flashlight in front of their feet to light their path. Just like a flashlight, the Bible shows us where to go. Let's listen to it now.

You could also introduce the story by relating the Bible passage to its context or to lessons that have come before. For our lesson about the lame beggar, you might say,

> Today's lesson is from the fifth book of the New Testament. Let's name those first five books together: *Matthew, Mark, Luke, John, Acts!*

With grade-school children, it can help to show the kids how the story fits with other stories in the larger biblical narrative.[5] You could introduce the story of the lame beggar by saying,

After Jesus rose from the dead and ascended to the Father, the Holy Spirit came with power upon his disciples in Jerusalem. They taught all the people about him and did many miracles. *Listen to this story about one of those miracles.*

Once you've introduced the story, it's time to tell it. Children's ministry curriculum providers often include written Bible stories for younger age groups that have simple age-targeted vocabulary and sentence structure.[6] If your curriculum doesn't provide stories like this, you may want to choose a Bible storybook that retells individual Bible stories in age-appropriate language. Some of my favorites are *The Child's Story Bible* by Catherine Vos for middle elementary kids, Sally Lloyd-Jones's *The Jesus Storybook Bible* for younger elementary and older preschoolers, and my own *Beginner's Gospel Story Bible* for toddlers and young preschoolers.[7]

Young children learn through facial expression and interaction, so get familiar enough with the story during your preparation time to tell it to the boys and girls without reading it to them word for word. When telling the story itself, you're helping kids see *what* the story is about. Know the conflict, climax, and resolution of the story, and keep the four columns of your interpretation chart in mind as well. You'll also want to be familiar with the illustrations in the storybooks or any visuals provided by your curriculum. Use these to keep children's interest. A young child's attention span can be as low as one minute per year of age, so toddlers in particular have an attention span of three-to-seven minutes. Prepare well so that you can make the most of those precious minutes![8]

When teaching older kids, I encourage them to bring their Bibles and read along as we study the passage. Sometimes I'll call on children to read aloud. With both older and younger kids, it can be helpful to include one or two controlled responses. When teaching kids about Daniel and Nebuchadnezzar, I once heard one of our church's classroom teachers call boys and girls to respond by saying, "*Bad, bad, bullies*" every time the Babylonians were mentioned in the lesson. With our Acts 3 story, you could encourage the kids to remember the story's plot by repeating three L-words: *Lame* (the disabled man's condition), *Look* (Peter's command to the man), and *Leap* (the man's response to the miracle).[9] Repeat the key truth or a condensed version of it like "Jesus is better than money" throughout the story and add hand motions to make it memorable.

As you teach, be alert for any words that might be hard for a child to understand. Younger children and unchurched kids may not understand more technical Bible terms, so you'll need to define them clearly. You might refer to a catechism like the children's edition of the New City Catechism (newcitycatechism.com) to find simple kid-friendly definitions when you're teaching kids more complex concepts.[10] If you reference the fact that "Peter and John went up to the temple to pray" when telling the story, you may want to define prayer ("Prayer is pouring out your heart to God") especially if prayer will be emphasized as an application later on in the Look or Took sections of the lesson.

After telling the story, you'll want to have some Bible story review questions for the kids to help drive the truths home. In preschool classes, it's helpful to transition the kids from the story circle to classroom tables and even provide a small snack before beginning the review. I've found snack time and trips to the restroom—while I have a captive audience with kids standing in line—to be excellent times for reviewing the key truth and any memory work.

Look—Make a Connection to Real Life.

After the Book section, it's time for hands-on crafts and active games that make a connection to real life. The Look section is an opportunity to get each child's entire body involved in learning. For our lesson about the lame man at the temple, you might have a carry-your-friend relay race. After the race, help the kids see the connection to the story and think about how the key truth relates to their own lives. You might say,

> Today, we learned about a lame man who had crippled and crooked legs. What would life be like for you if you needed friends to carry you everywhere you went? The man's friends carried him to the temple gate every day to beg for money. But the man discovers that Jesus is better than money, because Jesus provided complete healing. *Because Jesus is better than money, we can trust him to heal our broken world.*

Every Look activity should relate to the Bible story's key truth and provide the kids an opportunity to think, talk, or practice common sense applications. In this way, the Look section answers the *how* question. Here is another activity you might include in your Acts 3 lesson plan if you are teaching grade-school children.

First, form the kids into groups and give each group some pages from an advertising mailer or retail store catalog. Next, assign each group a budgeted amount of board game money and guide the boys and girls to pick out the items they want to buy.

Make certain the budgeted amount of money seems like a large amount to an average child but is small enough that it will only purchase a few items from the advertisement. After each group makes their shopping list, talk about what the kids observed while making the budget. You might say:

> Money runs out fast, doesn't it? Some people think the problems in our broken world—problems like hunger and sickness—can be fixed if we only have enough money. But there isn't enough money to fix our broken world. *Jesus is better than money!* Instead of trusting in money, *we can trust Jesus to heal our world.*

With preschoolers, a simple hands-on craft often makes for an excellent Look activity. Every craft that young children make is a valuable reinforcement tool. It makes a statement to kids and parents about what was learned during class. Including a clear, simple message that encapsulates what you want them to remember is a great way to help the application stick.[11] For the Acts 3 passage, you might distribute a green crayon and one four-inch paper circle cut from light blue construction paper to each child. Guide preschoolers to draw and color green "continents" on the circle to make a paper map of the world. Then, distribute an adhesive bandage to each child and show them how to adhere it to the paper craft. On each "world with a Band-Aid" craft, write *Jesus heals our broken world.*

Took—Motivate Dynamic Change.

The last section of our lesson plan is the Took section. As I wrote above, the Took is similar to the Look, because both of these parts of the lesson focus on applying biblical truth to a child's life. However, the Took is different, because it *inspires* biblical living and answers the *what if* question by helping kids to imagine the influence following Christ will have on their lives and our world. If it wasn't abundantly clear in the Book section, it's time to clarify why this lesson is good news. Some Bible passages—a lesson on the Ten Commandments for instance—will emphasize the Bible's commands ("Do this!"). With these passages, spend some time during the Took section emphasizing how our obedience comes through the power of the Spirit. Other passages—like the Acts 3 text we've been thinking through—emphasize what God has done for us. In this case, it's good for the Took section to include a celebration of God's work of grace and an opportunity to put implications of the passage into practice.

On our Acts 3 lesson plan (chart 7.3), I've written down "prayer and praise piggy bank" in the final lower-left-hand *Took* quadrant. With this activity, we'll teach boys and girls about prayer by asking them to write down either one thing they want to ask God for or one thing they want to thank God for. We encourage each child to share their prayers or praises with the class and then drop them into a plastic piggy bank with the words "Prayer and Praise" taped to the side. When the activity is complete, we say,

> People keep their money safe in a bank. *But Jesus is better than money!* He changed the lame man's begging into praise. *We can put our trust in Jesus* by daily praying in his name. Prayer is pouring out our heart to God. When we pray, we ask for God's help, and we say thank you!

Chart 7.3

Lesson Plan Diagram for Acts 3:1–10

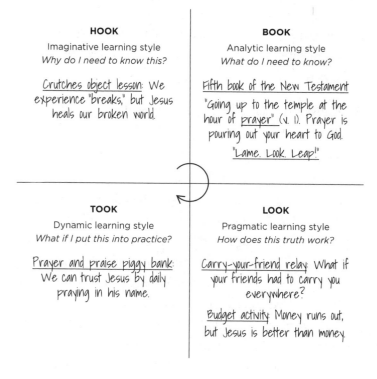

HOOK

Imaginative learning style
Why do I need to know this?

Crutches object lesson: We experience "breaks," but Jesus heals our broken world.

BOOK

Analytic learning style
What do I need to know?

Fifth book of the New Testament
"Going up to the temple at the hour of prayer" (v. 1). Prayer is pouring out your heart to God.
"Lame. Look. Leap!"

TOOK

Dynamic learning style
What if I put this into practice?

Prayer and praise piggy bank: We can trust Jesus by daily praying in his name.

LOOK

Pragmatic learning style
How does this truth work?

Carry-your-friend relay: What if your friends had to carry you everywhere?

Budget activity: Money runs out, but Jesus is better than money.

If you regularly teach kids at church, you may have noticed that coloring sheets and activity pages—staples of children's ministry curriculum—are conspicuously missing from my lesson plan. These tools can be helpful, but I try to save them for the margins of the lesson when I'm filling unplanned time, or I give them to kids who arrive early or who finish a craft activity more quickly than their peers. As Stephanie Carmichael observes, "The constant use of activity sheets can become regimental for teachers and boring for the children."[12] My goal is to always have these added resources on hand but move through the entire HBLT cycle without them. Remember, your goal is not to do every activity in the provided curriculum. Rather, it's to engage kids so that they learn God's word and see Christ through practice and experience.

A Creative Experience with an Educational and Relational Aim

When addressing a seminary class about how to create kid-friendly and engaging children's ministry games, one of the students objected, "That sounds like something you'd see on the children's cable channel, Nickelodeon. Is this just keeping kids entertained?" It was a good question. After all, I think the game in question did involve slime. Sometimes with kids' activities there is an entertainment factor, but now that I've had some time to reflect on that student's question, I'd say children's ministry activities *aren't* like Nickelodeon; they're more like PBS Kids. There's a goal in mind with a children's lesson that is larger than entertainment alone—one that is bigger than selling a product or a character. Like the interactive exhibits at a children's museum or the skits on Sesame Street, children's ministry is an experience, but it's an experience with an educational and relational aim. Dave Ainsworth, one of the pastors at Citizens Church in San Francisco, puts it this way: "Children's ministry done well leads kids to learn about Jesus through hands-on, real-life, engaging discovery."[13]

That's a great way of summing up what it means to connect kids to Jesus, but we're only halfway through our strategic pathway for children's discipleship. After you've created welcoming environments and crafted interactive and gospel-centered Bible lessons, how do you walk beside families to help them disciple their kids as they grow? In the next section, we'll explore what it means to help kids grow into a gospel-formed identity.

Reflection on Part 3

Connect Kids to Christ

TAKE A LOOK at the questions for reflection and evaluation below. Spend some time working through them and think about your own teaching.

Questions for Reflection and Evaluation

1. Review the three kinds of Bible stories in chapter 5. When you prepare a lesson, which type do you typically gravitate toward?

2. Read the following Bible passages out loud one at a time. For each of the stories, fill in an interpretation chart (blank sample on page 140). Work through each section of the chart by answering each question. Work slowly. Soulful reflections usually come with time. After answering each question, craft a memorable key truth statement. Then, if you are working

through this book with a group, discuss your observations and reflections.

Numbers 21:4–9	Matthew 1:18–24
1 Kings 10:1–13	Mark 4:36–41
2 Chronicles 33:1–20	Revelation 4:1–5:14

- **The Need.** Who in this story *needs* the gospel?

- **God's Actions.** What is *God* doing for his people in this story? In stories from the New Testament, you might ask, "What does this story teach us about who Jesus is or what he has done?"

- **Good News!** How does God do the same for us—only better—*in Jesus*? For New Testament stories, you might ask, "How does this story show us that Jesus is better than anything else?"

- **Believe It!** How does *believing* this good news change the way we live?

3. Choose one of the Bible passages above and create a sample lesson plan for your class using the lesson plan diagram on page 141. After writing out your lesson plan, evaluate it by answering the following questions:

- **Hook:** Is it engaging? Does the activity or object lesson work for your class size? Does it distract from the summary statement of your lesson, or does it support it? Does it provide a clear transition to the Book section?

- **Book:** Are you ready to help kids see each key plot movement in the Bible study? Are you ready to explain and define any difficult concepts or words in language that is age-appropriate? Do you have visuals, interactive questions, or controlled responses ready to help you keep the kids' attention? Are you ready to repeat the summary statement as you teach? Will kids walk away with clarity about how this story points to Jesus?

- **Look:** What should the kids do in response to the lesson? How can they apply this truth? Are you reinforcing these applications with hands-on crafts, practical activities, or active games that involve kids' heads, hearts, and hands?

- **Took:** Do these activities help kids imagine the influence following Christ can have on their lives and our world? Do they inspire grace-motivated obedience by pointing back to the motivation we find in the gospel or forward to the implications of the gospel?

For Further Study

Carmichael, Stephanie. *Their God Is So Big: Teaching Sunday School to Young Children.* Kingsford, NSW, Australia: Matthias Media, 2000.

Klumpenhower, Jack. *Show Them Jesus: Teaching the Gospel to Kids.* Greensboro: New Growth, 2014.

LeFever, Marlene D. *Learning Styles: Reaching Everyone God Gave You to Teach.* Colorado Springs: NexGen, 2004.

Richards, Lawrence O. and Gary J. Bredfeldt. *Creative Bible Teaching.* Revised and expanded. Chicago: Moody Press, 1998.

Interpretation Chart

Scripture Passage:

Because . . . (write a good-news statement here):

I can . . . (write a believe-it statement here):

The Need Who in this story needs good news?	God's Actions What is God doing for his people in this story?	Good News! How does God do the same for us—only better—in Jesus?	Believe It! How does believing this good news change the way we live?

Lesson Plan Diagram

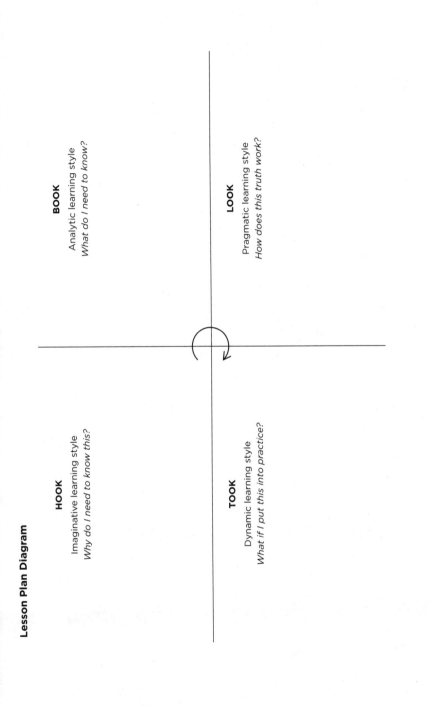

HOOK

Imaginative learning style
Why do I need to know this?

BOOK

Analytic learning style
What do I need to know?

LOOK

Pragmatic learning style
How does this truth work?

TOOK

Dynamic learning style
What if I put this into practice?

PART 4

GROW WITH KIDS
AND FAMILIES

8

Step-by-Step, Stage-by-Stage

*Helping Kids Embrace the
Gospel as They Grow*

A FOURTH-GRADE classroom at the church where I served was studying the ark of the covenant and the tabernacle. Over weeks, we dug into the Old Testament details—the tabernacle furniture and each of the prescribed sacrifices. Our teaching team complained about the lessons. If I'm honest, I struggled as their leader too. How could teaching something as theologically complex and gruesome as the sacrificial system benefit grade-school kids? After all, the bloody sacrifices ended with the death of Christ.

When we taught how the Israelites had received forgiveness and access to God by making sacrifices, one girl (we'll call her Sarah) said, "I wish we could still do that." We were shocked. Did I need to make a quick curriculum change? We teach with confidence that the Bible speaks to all ages, but it doesn't speak to all ages in the same way. I wondered if I had taught this ancient text to these young students in a sufficient way.

Sarah's story illustrates a key truth about children's ministry. We need to present engaging, Christ-centered lessons to children, but they also need to be *developmentally appropriate*. In this chapter, I want to help you think about this important concern by giving you an overview of early childhood development from birth to age ten. We'll look at these years in four stages—the infant, toddler, preschool, and early grade-school years. For each stage, we'll explore how a child's cognitive and relational development influences her spiritual life, how our children's ministry environments should adapt, and what encouragements are helpful to give parents and caregivers at each stage.

Infants (Birth–24 Months): Learning to Trust

If you've worked with kids for any time at all, you've probably noticed that changes come quickly in early childhood. Tiny babies in particular change rapidly. Early in this stage, a baby will suck his thumb and mimic his caretakers' facial expressions. But by three months or so, the child begins to recognize his environment in a more observable way. A child will touch soft things or squeeze a toy. The more infants grow, the more they begin to be interested in things and explore their environments. By eight or nine months, children develop what psychologists describe as *object permanence*, as the children begin to look around for hidden objects.[1]

Infants also begin to imitate or make representations of things they have seen—like waving Hi or Bye. Before they've reached age two, infants are able to work simple combinations in their minds: *I can put down the bucket to pick up the toy*. Pretend play begins as well. A child will rock a doll and tuck it into bed. Kids will also begin to see an object not only as what it is but also as

THE INFANT STAGE[2]

Infants . . .

- recognize human faces and voices, especially primary caregivers (0–4 weeks).
- begin to show a preferential attachment for a primary caregiver (1–3 months).
- explore the world by using their senses to take in their environments (1–3 months).
- play baby games like peek-a-boo (3–4 months).
- demonstrate motor skills like supporting their heads and necks (around 3 months) and simple eye-hand coordination (4–5 months).
- develop object permanence, the ability to understand that objects still exist when they are no longer visible (8–9 months).
- develop memory, demonstrated by recognizing a routine and experiencing stranger anxiety (8–10 months).
- learn by imitating caregivers (10–12 months)—waving Hi and Bye.
- babble to communicate (4–6 months) and learn to speak first words (9–12 months).
- begin to crawl, cruise, and then walk (7–14 months).
- begin to play by pretending (12–18 months).

what it could be. For example, a child may pick up a toy block and pretend it's a telephone.[3]

We're thrilled to see babies soak up life and learn new skills during this earliest stage, but it's easy to miss the way they learn. Infants perceive life primarily through an emotional grid, not a logical one. What a child most needs at this stage is loving and attentive care. Karyn Henley reminds us, "When the infant is hungry, we feed him. When he's cold, we wrap him in a blanket. When his diaper is wet, we put a clean diaper on him. He learns that he can trust us to take care of him."[4]

As infant children are nurtured and cared for, they learn that while they may experience momentary discomfort, everything will work out right because there is someone taking care of them. During this stage, it's important for a child's primary caregivers to be reliable and available. When caregivers are consistently unavailable, a child learns to avoid trusting others. When caregivers are consistently unreliable, a child can grow to be deeply insecure. In fact, some developmental difficulties can be traced to children not coming to see that the world is a safe place.[5]

God designed the family so that parents' tender, available, and consistent care for us during our earliest years would mirror God the Father's care for his people. Consider how God loved and cared for our first parents perfectly. He provided Adam with everything he needed—a place to live (Gen. 2:8), food (1:29; 2:9), water (2:10–14), responsibility (1:28; 2:15), boundaries for his protection (2:16–17), and even companionship (2:18, 21–25). God shows this same kind of intimacy and love to every child from conception (Ps. 139:13–18).

How can parents and church nursery workers model God's trustworthy care to the youngest children? How do we help infants learn to trust? Here are two encouragements:

- **Be nurturing and available.** Your ability to trust that God is unchanging in his love and care was developed before ten months of age. So it's important for caregivers to show babies consistent affection through appropriate physical touch, eye contact, focused attention, and a predictable routine. A consistent and nurturing atmosphere is equally important in our ministry environments. Little additions like soft music and lighting can make the church nursery a warmer place, but most important is that it's led by people who are calm, joyful, and gentle.

- **Plant seeds of faith.** We should also encourage both parents and nursery workers to introduce infants to God in simple but intentional ways. Though a baby may not understand the words "Jesus loves you" or "God made these little toes," we shouldn't underestimate what God might choose to do through our speaking or singing simple truths over them. We can say to babies, "I'm taking care of you, because God takes care of you," or "I love you, because Jesus loves you."[6]

Toddlers (Ages 2–3): Growing in Joy and Confidence

Have you ever played hide and seek with a toddler? You announce, "Go and hide!" Then, the two-year-old quickly shuts his eyes and throws his hands over his face. He thinks that because he can't see you, you can't see him either.

In the toddler stage, children are really coming into their own. By eighteen months, toddlers use words, numbers, and even toys to communicate. They'll demonstrate that a picture of a dog, the printed word "DOG," and saying the word "dog" all represent a dog. But young toddlers aren't just learning new words and how different symbols can stand for the same concept. They also manipulate symbols through creative play. Whereas an older infant might pick up a block and pretend it's a telephone, a three-year-old will pretend a set of checkers is a tray of cookies. This is because toddlers are growing to understand themselves and their place in the world. By naming things ("This checker is a cookie"), a toddler is saying, *I know what's up. I can make my way.*

When toddlers are developing appropriately, they're also learning many new skills and want to do things for themselves. As Henley observes, "Adults can look for things the child can do on her own. Show the child what she can do: brush her teeth, wash her face, pick up toys, put on Velcro-fastened shoes, and many other things."[7] As a child learns to be independent in these small ways, she feels a sense of pride: *Look what I can do!*

Toddler-age children are so focused on growing as individuals that they have trouble walking in someone else's shoes. That's why playing hide and seek can be so funny. Toddlers are what psychologists call *egocentric.* This is not selfishness necessarily—though, because kids are sinners, they certainly battle selfishness too. Rather, when we talk about a toddler being egocentric, it's a matter of developmental perspective. They aren't quite ready or able to see things from another person's point of view. Teachers must understand that twos and threes are typically not ready for group activities. They demonstrate what's called *parallel play*—playing near other children but not necessarily with them in a cooperative way.

Of course, an egocentric perspective and greater confidence in new skills can come with difficulties. Children in the toddler stage also begin to exert their will. They quickly learn to say, *No.* This means caregivers sometimes have to walk the difficult road between affirming the child's new abilities and teaching him his limitations. After all, there are many things young toddlers are not capable of doing, and there are many things they should not be allowed to do. Parents and caregivers must learn to allow the

THE TODDLER STAGE[8]

Toddlers . . .

- struggle to think abstractly. They need simple and concrete examples.
- have an attention span of three-to-seven minutes.
- are learning lots of new words. They now know words for emotions and can also learn Bible words.
- may experience separation anxiety when leaving preferred caregivers but also like to actively explore new environments.
- are growing in independence. They are learning new skills such as holding utensils and writing tools, pedaling, dressing themselves, and using the toilet on their own.
- have difficulty seeing the world from another person's point of view (egocentrism).
- like to make friends and play near other children (parallel play) but young toddlers struggle to play with other children cooperatively.
- begin to test authority and demonstrate their own will. They need clear structure and consequences for disobedience.
- recite songs, rhymes, and simple stories.
- have limited small motor skills. They'll need lots of help when coloring and gluing.

children in their care to express their will and emotions but in a respectful way. This allows them to grow in confidence and independence but still under the authority, care, and protection of the adults in their lives.

How can parents and children's minsters help toddlers have joy in God as they're coming into their own? Here are a few suggestions:

- **Cultivate joy in learning new skills.** The excitement toddlers have about learning new skills is right and good. Don't squash it. Parents need to cheer when they "go in the potty" and dress themselves. Classroom teachers can enjoy kids' skills and uniqueness as God's creation (Ps. 139:13–18), but we should go beyond merely praising them and praise God for them. "I'm so glad God brought you to our class today!"

- **Make learning active.** Toddlers are naturally curious and wiggly. When adults are merely talking at them, it's easy for something across the room to draw their attention away and send their small bodies off for a personal investigation. For this reason, two- and three-year-old children need to become physically involved in the lesson by doing hands-on crafts, controlled responses with the story, hand motions with music, or by playing active games (see chapter 7).

- **Root their identity in the gospel story.** A toddler's language abilities are exploding. Most two-year-old children can say around two hundred words; before their fourth birthdays, they'll know nearly 1,500.[9] A child may learn important words like "Bible," "prayer," or even "Jesus" for the first time during the toddler years. Around age two, toddlers start making up stories about daily events.[10] Hearing and telling stories gives young kids a sense of rooted identity. So don't underestimate the influence you have when teaching toddlers.

Preschoolers (Ages 4–5): Developing Initiative and Conscience

Preschool children are explorers, pushing limits and experimenting with life to see what will happen. One healthy way preschool children explore the world is by using their imaginations. During the toddler years, a child moves from literal interpretations of objects to understanding symbols; by age five, children are exploring the difference between fantasy play—elaborate stories and imaginary friends—and reality. In these years, children begin to act out elaborate stories, often by dressing up as their favorite characters from books or television.

A preschool child's expanding boundaries stretch her relationships too. She moves from parallel play to *associative play*. No longer content to sit next to a friend while both color or play with blocks, a four-year-old girl may say to a friend, "You be the mommy, and I'll be the little baby," or, "You be the store man, and I'll come buy some food."

As preschoolers push their limits, they'll sometimes encounter boundaries. They get frustrated when they don't get what they want, and they feel guilty when they break a rule. When a child is disobedient, the feeling of guilt is appropriate, but it's important for parents and caregivers not to put so many restrictions in place that a child's curiosity is discouraged.

Adults certainly shouldn't let a child do anything he wants, but we should have an encouraging attitude toward the child's God-given desire to know and explore. Parents need to learn encouraging ways to say no. For example, "I'm glad you want to dig in the dirt. But now is not the time," or, "This is not a good place to dig. Here's a better place." Giving chores to a young child is another helpful way to channel the child's initiative and help communicate that he or she has a purpose in the world, in his family, and in the classroom. How can we help preschoolers grow both in initiative and obedience? We

THE PRESCHOOL STAGE[11]

Preschoolers . . .
- speak clearly, using complex sentences and sharing simple stories.
- demonstrate a greater use of imagination—exploring the difference between fantasy and reality. Play-by-play self-talk is common during dress-up or role-playing games.
- are more aware of feelings and can begin to demonstrate empathy.
- are becoming more social and play *with* friends (associative play), not just near them.
- are learning cooperation, sharing, and how to take turns.
- have an attention span of 10–15 minutes.
- demonstrate an awareness of gender and gender roles in play and peer relationships.
- typically become aware of prejudiced racial stereotypes, particularly minority children.
- can follow multiple-step directions and have a growing sense of time.
- need structure and can follow simple rules.
- begin to test authority, demonstrating their own will.
- consciences are undeveloped; good and bad behavior are often understood through attached consequences.

must imitate our Father's love and discipline with preschool children. Here's how:

- **Be consistent.** Preschoolers need simple repeated rules and predictable schedules that are consistently followed. It's important for classroom teachers to be prepared and organized, structured and well-paced. Half of classroom management with young children is knowing exactly what you are going to do. Some of the best preschool teachers I know have only four simple rules in their classroom. They use interactive hand motions to remind the young children of these expectations: (1) first-time obedience (*hold up one finger*); (2) teacher's hand up means to be quiet (*hand up*); (3) "give me five" means to give me your full attention (*five fingers* for all five senses—though the teachers I know have joked with their classes that tasting and smelling aren't necessary); and (4) keep your hands and bodies to yourself (*wiggle hands out and then quickly pull them in*).

- **Appeal to their developing conscience.** Young preschoolers still depend on rules—and the enforcement of those rules—to guide them in knowing and choosing between what's right and wrong. Their conscience—the ability to identify and describe our positive and negative internal judgments about ideas, actions, and situations[12]—is undeveloped but forming. Caregivers can appeal to the child's developing conscience by using phrases such as "Jesus is sad when we disobey him." In this way, we can help kids form an internal sense of right and wrong that will stay with them as they grow.

- **Appeal to the joy found in exploring the world God's way.** We need to help kids understand that life works out best and we experience joy when we follow God's commands (John 15:10–11). I've heard parents and children's ministry workers say, "Kids need to respect authority. They don't always need a reason." That may be true. Certainly, I want my daughters to jump at my word if they are in imminent danger. But regularly giving them the reasons behind the expectation helps them to *own* God's loving purposes—and my loving purposes—for themselves.

Early Grade School (Ages 6–10): Humor, Competition, and Critical Thinking

What has ears but can't hear? *Corn!* Why don't lobsters share? *Because they're shellfish.* What did the egg say to the frying pan? *You crack me up.* Early grade-school kids love these kinds of jokes! By age seven, they are able to reflect on more abstract ideas, and they are also amply verbal. They're learning all sorts of skills in school related to reading, writing, and speaking.[13]

At this age, a child is able to spell out words, work math problems, and read books. Throughout this stage, kids' interpretive ability increases as well. Early grade-school kids are able to answer who, what, where, and when questions, but they're not always able to make the intellectual leap to answering why questions. They may struggle to understand the more abstract motives or reasons for a person's actions.

Fantasy play continues from ages six to nine but typically with dolls or action figures rather than dress-up and role-play games. As kids move toward the teen years, imaginative play is replaced by hobbies and sports. As kids in middle childhood develop physically—gaining adult teeth, growing appetites, and improved coordination and strength—they become more active and competitive.

Often younger elementary kids compete and perform to gain approval and affirmation from parents and other adults. But increasingly during this stage peer influences begin to matter more and more. School-age children are more aware of other people

THE EARLY GRADE-SCHOOL STAGE[14]

Kids in early grade school . . .

- have an increased ability to recall events and remember sequence. They spell out words and read books. They think more systematically and are able to generalize what is learned.
- continue fantasy play—typically with dolls and action figures (ages 6–9).
- grow up physically with adult teeth, growing appetites, and improved coordination and strength.
- gain confidence and security as they develop new skills. They demonstrate greater self-control and an ability to think before acting.
- improve handwriting and hand-eye coordination. They are able to draw more complex pictures with objects, people, animals (ages 7–9).
- have varied attention spans that average fifteen minutes between ages 7–9 and twenty minutes between ages 10–12.
- will often prefer a same-sex peer group (ages 6–9). May have a "best friend." Around age ten, a child may have more interest in the opposite sex and experience his or her first "crush."
- can enter puberty as early as age nine. Girls typically develop more quickly than boys.
- want to please parents and other adults, but peer influence begins to shape likes and dislikes.
- have a view of the world that extends beyond a black-white or right-wrong perspective and beyond their personal experiences.
- can more clearly distinguish between will, actions, and motives (around age 10).

and themselves as members of a group, and they have an increasing desire to be accepted by their peers. They're typically fearful of looking foolish, making a mistake, or being embarrassed. It's essential for caregivers not only to celebrate kids' accomplishments but to show them unconditional love and affection, making sure to avoid tying love to particular behaviors or skills.

We must also be aware that grade-school children are critical thinkers. We shouldn't be surprised when they begin to see the brokenness of our fallen world. Kids enter middle childhood with a rule-oriented mindset and a strong sense of fairness—even Pharisaical fairness: "follow the rules and you are good" instead of "Jesus makes us good."[15] But as kids head toward the teen years, they often begin questioning rules and become more critical of parents, teachers, and one another.

How do we shepherd kids' hearts during this stage of humor, competition, and critical thinking?

- **Encourage kids to read and study the Bible.** There's a tremendous variation in reading and writing skills during grade school. In the first few years of this stage, teaching must be structured to accommodate both readers and non-readers. But even with six- and seven-year-olds, basic Bible reading skills such as memorizing the books of the Bible in order or learning how to look up a Scripture passage can be taught. As kids become readers, we should encourage them to bring their Bibles to church and emphasize the discovery of truths from Scripture through activities that highlight comparing, contrasting, and analyzing. By fifth grade, kids can dig into the big themes of the Scriptures presented through units of Bible study that are organized historically and chronologically.[16]

- **Help kids see their sinful hearts, and call them to trust Christ.**
  As grade-school kids grow in critical thinking, they'll have a tendency to judge other people's values and sinful behavior. While it's important for us to teach kids God's law of love, we also want to help kids identify their own sins and the inconsistency that exists between what they say and what they do. When kids begin to see their sin, we must be ready to share with them about God's grand plan to rescue and restore our broken world. And we must call them to respond to Christ with faith.

That's what Sarah, the little girl I wrote about at the beginning of this chapter, needed to hear in the moment when she wanted to kill a lamb. It's true that at age nine she was only beginning to reflect on abstract concepts. But when our children's ministry teachers talked with Sarah and her parents after class, it turned out she'd said some harsh words to her younger brother earlier that week.

As Sarah's class dug into the Bible and studied our need for blood atonement, she felt her guilt vividly. Sarah found the concrete offer of forgiveness promised through blood sacrifice to be appealing. She wanted to kill a lamb and be done with her sin. The morning Sarah expressed this desire was an opportunity for our children's ministry team to draw near to her in love, share the gospel, and call her to respond to Christ.

Our team of teachers explained how Jesus has already made the sacrifice Sarah longed for, and he has done it once and for all. They clarified the truth of the good news, and they pleaded with Sarah to believe it. She didn't receive Christ's comfort for several more years after that conversation, but the team called her to respond in faith that day, and I'm glad they did. With loving care and wisdom about how kids grow, we can confidently share the good news with children. We do so with knowledge that God is at work, growing them up step-by-step and stage-by-stage.

Catechizing the YouTube Generation

*An Ancient Path toward a
Gospel-Formed Life*

IN FEBRUARY 2020, comedy duo Rhett McLaughlin and Link Neal, hosts of the Good Mythical Morning YouTube channel and the Ear Biscuits podcast, went public with their deconversion. They posted a series of recorded videos that walked fans through their reasons for leaving the Christian faith. Many believing kids were stunned. "Several people reached out to me personally," wrote apologetics blogger, Alisa Childers, "including pastors who reported that the faith of several kids in their youth groups was rocked by the broadcasts, leaving them shaken and doubting."[1]

Rhett and Link's platform wasn't merely built on clean middle school humor—an annual Halloween candy bracket challenge, satirical songs, and duct-taping themselves together. They'd also publicly identified with Christ. Both served on staff with the college ministry, Cru. And more recently they were featured as "The Fabulous Bentley Brothers" singing songs about the Bible in Phil Vischer's *What's in the Bible?* video series for children.

What changed Rhett and Link's minds about Christianity? As Rhett tells it, he began with questions about the Bible's relationship to science, the age of the earth, and evolution. This grew into doubts about the historicity of the resurrection and the justice of hell and final judgment. Rhett and Link also felt discomfort with the Bible's sexual ethics, which they perceive as oppressive to women and their LGBTQ+ friends. The complaints Rhett and Link raise about Christianity aren't new, but, as Childers writes, "the same timeworn skepticism the church has interacted with since its inception is given a fresh dose of potency when delivered to a whole new generation by cool and funny guys who've become a fixture of their childhood."[2]

It's not that youth ministers couldn't find good arguments to counter Rhett and Link's skepticism. There are lots of great books that defend the Christian faith by authors like Lee Strobel and Tim Keller. The trouble is that Rhett and Link hadn't simply won the youth group kids' minds; Rhett and Link had won their hearts. The two comedians are lovable, and the youth who follow them are part of a loyal community whose thinking, affections, and habits of life had been shaped by coming back to the duo's YouTube channel day after day.

Teach, Know, Live

When families become regular parts of a church fellowship, local church leaders have a responsibility to encourage them along in their faith journey. We need a discipleship strategy that seeks to shape kids' doctrine, passions, and patterns of life. Chapter 8 discussed how we can call kids to developmentally appropriate faith responses. In addition to teaching content *to* children and crafting engaging and age-appropriate lessons that are specifically *for* children, we must walk *with* children in their discipleship journey.[3] In this chapter, I'll explore how we can equip parents with resources and rhythms that will help them walk with their children on a path of discipleship. Psalm 78 gives us a three-stage framework for training the next generation in the faith. Let's take a look at verses 5–7:

> He established a testimony in Jacob
>   and appointed a law in Israel,
> which he commanded our fathers
>   to *teach* to their children,
> that the next generation might *know* them,
>   the children yet unborn,
> and arise and tell them to their children,
>   so that they should set their hope in God
> and not forget the works of God,
>   but *keep* his commandments.

After giving Israelite parents and the covenant community as a whole the responsibility to train the next generation (see chapter 1), the psalmist goes on to describe what that training process entailed. God wanted Israel's kids to be *taught* his law and testimony so that they would *know* his commands and his story. He wanted Israelite children to come to know him as well—to set their hope in him and not forget his works. The goal was for each successive generation to grow into adults who embodied and *kept* God's commands and then passed them along to the generation after them.[4]

Let's look at this discipleship process step-by-step and consider what following it might entail for moms and dads who are raising kids in the age of YouTube.

Teaching the Basics

No child who is learning mathematics jumps straight into quadratic equations. She must first learn to count, then add, subtract, multiply, and divide. Once the basics are mastered, she will encounter the complexities of algebra, geometry, and calculus. The same is true with our faith. We don't dive into the complexities of the Trinity with preschoolers. We first introduce them to the basics of the Christian life by telling simple Bible stories, memorizing short verses, and rehearsing bedtime prayers.

One great tool that can help parents with the task of teaching the basics is a catechism.[5] I admit that the word "catechism" and the practice of catechizing comes with some baggage. Next to Rhett and Link's daily videos, a catechism may seem quirky, outdated, and rigid. If you are from a Reformed or Lutheran background, you may remember studying catechism in confirmation classes. Presbyterians will at least know that the answer to the question "What is the chief end of man?" is "to glorify God and enjoy him forever." Other readers may never have heard of catechism at all.

The English word catechism comes from the Greek word *katācheō*, which means to teach or instruct. The Greek word is used for any kind of teaching or instruction (Luke 1:4; Acts

18:25), but early in church history it came to refer to the teaching of new converts, who were taught the basics of Christianity by memorizing questions and answers about church doctrine and practice.[6] Catechisms as they're used today are just that—a series of questions and answers used to teach basic Bible truth.

The roots of this method go even further back than the early church. When God rescued Israel from Egypt, he gave them laws, ceremonies, and sacrifices to help them remember his great rescue. God had kids in mind when he gave the law. We can see this in the way God anticipated their questions. In passages like Exodus 12:26–27; Exodus 13:14–16; and Joshua 4:6–7, we find a pattern like this one: *When your children ask you, "What does this ceremony mean to you?" then tell them* . . .

God created kids with curiosity and a sense of wonder. When they asked questions about his laws or the Passover celebration, God wanted Israelite parents to be prepared. In each of these passages, he gave them a simple script for answering their kids' questions. In Exodus 12:27, the answer went like this: "It is the sacrifice of the LORD's Passover, for he passed over the houses of the people of Israel in Egypt, when he struck the Egyptians but spared our houses." God instructed parents to put this script to memory, so that they'd always be ready with an answer—one that explained to their children how the annual celebration was rooted in God's big redemption plan.

When our daughters were small, we'd turn on worship music in their bedrooms to help them fall asleep each night. One of the albums we selected was a children's catechism set to music. Before they could understand what they were singing, our girls learned to rehearse the strangeness and beauty of Christian doctrine summarized in the Apostles' Creed, the Bible's ethic summarized in the Ten Commandments, and Jesus's model of communing with God in the Lord's Prayer.

The best catechisms major on these gospel basics—creed, commandments, and prayer. They help kids learn what Dorothy Sayers describes as the "grammar" of the faith.[7] The Gospel Coalition's *New City Catechism* follows this pattern, and its children's version is simple enough to begin learning with a toddler.[8]

A catechism can form the framework for an excellent children's ministry curriculum as well. In one church where I served, the children's ministry curriculum we adopted walked through the Bible chronologically, but we supplemented these lessons by rehearsing a monthly catechism question in our large group gatherings. One of our volunteers created a fun riff that he'd play on his guitar each week to introduce the catechism question. The kids would dance to the tune then shout out "Catechism!" as the riff ended. Then, we'd repeat the question and answer as a call and response. It's one way we sought to make learning the basic doctrines of the faith a joy.

A *Knowledge* of God Inspired by a Passion for His Story

My grandfather's generation sat at the breakfast table reading the morning newspaper. Generation Z—kids born from 1996 to 2014, a group that's now the largest segment of the US population (24.3 percent)[9]—gets up to check Snapchat and YouTube. Ninety-two percent of teens go online daily.[10] And it's no wonder. The internet is the place kids go to achieve. It's not just that assignments and quizzes are online at Google Classroom or Code.org.

Youth are also looking for achievement through the world of social media.

When they go online, today's teens are doing what kids have done for generations before them; they're trying to fit in. "Because of this," writes Danah Boyd, sociotechnical researcher for Microsoft, "teens are inclined to present a side of themselves that will be well received by these peers."[11] In other words, the number of comments, likes, and follows young people have—like the clothes they wear or where they sit in the school cafeteria—communicates something about their social standing.

What's different for youth today is that smartphones have made the social pressure to fit in portable. As a result, the work of managing friends' impressions online can become a full-time job. Some kids embrace managing their platform with a passion. The likes and love from friends bring confidence and pleasure, and the joy they find in social platforms isn't all self-indulgent.

Being socially connected has had the added advantage of helping many young people develop empathy, realism, and a sense of purpose. The growth of the online world has exposed them to more diverse friendships, connecting them with others from a variety of ethnic backgrounds and cultural experiences. Gen Z is more aware of suffering and injustice in the world, and they're often ready to use social media to share passion about their favored causes.

But for every kid online happily posting selfies or crusading for social justice, there's another who has been a victim of cyberbullying or who has grown disillusioned. "Likes" come to be superficial. And if voices of justice remain online and unheard in day-to-day life, they seem superficial too.

How can the church respond to Generation Z's passion for affirmation, acceptance, and justice? I believe we should see it as an opportunity. After all, we're all made for more. Both the joys we experience in this life and our unfulfilled desires reveal a deep longing for God's kingdom.

Kids are longing for holistic covenant love and kingdom justice that transcends their daily experience. They're looking for commitment that's more lasting than a social network can offer. They're looking for a place where the work of justice is done and not merely talked about. That's why it's essential for us to do more than teach them the basics of the faith, we need to help them embrace the love that's better than life (Ps. 63:3) and the true justice which will one day roll across the world like ocean waves (Amos 5:24).

As Champ Thornton encourages us, we need to help them make the connections between "the goodness of God and the wonders of science, the vigor of athletics, and the joys of language."[12] This will help them to see that Christ isn't merely a chosen part of life; he is our life (Col. 3:4).

Kids need the Bible's better—more holistic and more transcendent—story:

- *It's a story that shows us a redemptive love that transcends this life's superficial experiences.* It will show kids that their worth is not tied to comments or likes, because all people are valued as image bearers of the Creator King.
- *It's a story that shows kids a Savior who stood starkly against a superficial culture.* A bold church that knows and loves him will stand out today as well. Loving Jesus publicly will be socially awkward

at times. Teaching kids about sins and talking about hell and judgment are nearly always socially awkward. But loving the next generation means speaking the truth even when it seems strange.

• *It's a story that explains the world's brokenness in ways that are more contemporary than we sometimes care to admit.* If we open the Bible with our kids to narratives from Judges and Kings, we can help them see that the religious pluralism and sexual confusion they encounter in their friend groups doesn't take God by surprise. In our children's departments, we'll need to be careful to make the stories age appropriate. But preteens often see all the brokenness on social media already. So, we shouldn't be afraid to show it to them in God's Word.

This is the story Generation Z needs to hear. And they need to hear how we've embraced it personally. That means that as parents and church leaders we must confess our own personal and corporate sins. Gen Z kids need to see a church that is actively repenting from a history of racial discrimination and a lack of concern for the poor. Kids need parents who are gracious enough to ask forgiveness when they lose their temper or speak out of turn.

If kids are going to put down their phones and find deeper satisfaction in Jesus, they need to see parents and ministry leaders who are passionate about telling the big story and modeling the story's character. They need to see us model this passion day after day.

Living the Story as a Matter of Habit

Allen Curry, a professor and Christian educator, compares a children's ministry curriculum plan to a group of preschoolers making a string of beads. To make this necklace craft, it's first necessary to have the beads.[13] For Curry, the beads represent the basic Bible stories, memory verses, catechism questions, and prayers that children learn when they are young.

When you give young children beads, they'll sometimes begin to sort them by size and color or arrange them into patterns. Similarly, as kids grow and gain familiarity with basic Bible content, they begin to learn something about how the Bible's basic truths relate to one another. For instance, kids might learn to think about Bible stories chronologically, "Abraham lived after Noah," or thematically, "Joshua and Gideon both show us something about courage."

To complete the craft, you also need a string that holds the beads together. In Christian discipleship, the storyline of redemption—the gospel—is that scarlet thread. Seeing Jesus throughout the Bible is, in some ways, the capstone of discipleship, but there's one more step. A necklace is meant to be worn. And that's the true goal of discipleship. We want students to so own Christ's story that it influences their character, affections, and habits of life.

Much of how we respond to life is rooted in our habits, and there may be no time when habit and tradition show up more clearly than at the holidays. We gather with family for turkey and fixings on Thanksgiving, and then settle in the family room to watch football over the course of the weekend. We set up the tree, hang the stockings, and turn on the Martina McBride Christmas album (at least those are the habits in our home).

It shouldn't be a surprise to us that when God commanded the Israelites to pass down his law and testimony, he encouraged them to make their discipleship responsibility a matter of habit and celebration. God didn't simply give Israelite parents doctrinal summaries. He also gave them annual festivals. Leviticus 23 outlines a series of celebrations from Passover to the Feast of Weeks that helped Israelite families rehearse the journey from Exodus to Sinai every year.

New Testament believers aren't required to celebrate annual religious festivals (Col. 2:16), but we do want our personal story to be shaped by Christ's story. One way many Christians throughout history have practiced this is by letting Christ's life shape their church calendar—not just at Christmas and Easter but throughout the year. The movements of the historic Christian calendar mark the milestones of Jesus's earthly ministry—from the promise of his coming at Advent through his resurrection at Easter and the coming of the Holy Spirit at Pentecost.

I'm part of a church community that follows the liturgical calendar, and for that I'm thankful. Rejoicing in Jesus's birth by singing "Silent Night" at midnight each Christmas Eve and remembering how he was tempted in the wilderness on Ash Wednesday morning are now part of an annual routine for my oldest daughter. She looks forward to those events each year. But even if you don't fast during Lent or cap off the twelve days of Christmas with an Epiphany feast, I think you'll share my conviction that the goal of generational discipleship is for our kids to have a gospel-formed identity. We want our kids' pattern of life to be shaped by Christ's story.

A 2017 Lifeway Research project revealed some family culture factors that when present during the childhood years contributed to the spiritual health of surveyed young adults. Bible reading was the most important, but there were others including prayer,

GOSPEL-FORMED IDENTITY

Gospel-formed identity—the goal of generational discipleship is for our kids' thinking, affections, and habits of life to be shaped by Christ's story.

service in a local church, mission trips, community service, and listening to Christian music.[14]

James K. A. Smith reminds us that "being disciples of Jesus is not primarily a matter of getting the right ideas and doctrines and beliefs into your head in order to guarantee proper behavior; rather it's being the kind of person who loves rightly—who loves God and neighbor and is oriented toward the world by the primacy of that love."[15] Our hearts' passions aren't shaped by knowing doctrine alone. Rather, as the Lifeway study reveals, the pathway to a gospel-formed life is laid with intentional habits and rhythms at an early age.

Matt Chandler and Adam Griffin encourage each family in their church to cultivate a culture of discipleship through *intentional times* (e.g., family worship, one-on-one Bible study, family movie nights, etc.), through capturing and leveraging *teachable moments* as they come, and through making and marking significant *spiritual milestones* in a child's life (e.g., child dedications, conversion, first Bible, a rite of passage trip, or a first paycheck).[16]

It can be tempting for children's ministers and parents to overthink family discipleship—to try to build another volunteer-laden ministry program or a series of parenting classes. But it's more

TIMES, MOMENTS, MILESTONES[17]

Family Discipleship Time. Creating intentional time built into the rhythms of the family's life for the purpose of thinking about, talking about, and living out the gospel.

Family Discipleship Moments. Capturing and leveraging opportunities in the course of everyday life for the purpose of gospel-centered conversations.

Family Discipleship Milestones. Making and marking occasions to celebrate and commemorate significant spiritual milestones of God's work in the life of the family and child.

effective for ministry leaders to look at their community's annual calendar to identify times and seasons when families already have regular habits and rhythms in place. Then, parents can be encouraged to add a dose of intentional discipleship to what they're already doing.

After all, most of us learn best when we're building new habits on top of the routines we're already keeping. Here are some examples. A local church might hand out a Bible to each second-grade child at the beginning of the school year, give parents some family fun ideas during the summer, or distribute a devotional that helps parents teach their kids in the weeks leading up to Christmas or Easter.

For me, the Advent season has been the time when I've learned the most about family discipleship. Years ago, a pastor shared a website with our family that had twenty-five Christmas devotionals.

Each one told the story of a person from Jesus's family tree. My wife then found a similar book that had paper ornaments to correspond with the devotionals. We cut out the ornaments and read the stories to our daughters.

By reading through the Bible stories and slowly decorating a tiny one-and-a-half-foot discount store Christmas tree, we developed a habit of reading the Bible together as a family—one that stuck with us beyond that first year. I'm not always consistent with family devotions, but the Advent season always seems to draw our family back to time in the Word together. After all, that little tree and some felt ornaments (that have replaced the paper ones) are kept with our boxes of Christmas decorations. When our youngest sees them, she asks, "Which Advent book are we reading this year?" Then, as a matter of habit, we're beckoned back to our annual rhythm of discipleship—the kind the prophet Jeremiah described as an "ancient path" (Jer. 6:16).

Discipling the YouTube Generation with a Better Story

When the "Please silence your electronic devices" message appears on the big screen, people seem to instantly obey. Moments before, they were texting and posting pictures, but now they're putting their phones in airplane mode. Ironically, the middle school girl, an iconic representative of the most tech-savvy, hyper-connected generation in history, is elbowing her dad: "Put it away. The show's about to start." When they go to the theater, even the YouTube generation stops to sit still. They're transfixed by a story.

It's tempting to think that the only way to reach a hyper-connected generation is by making our children's and family ministry environments look more like YouTube—more wired, gamified, and image-rich. Some might say, "If we want the kids to put away their phones and tune in, we should take them to the movies." There's an element of truth in this, of course. Ministers should be mindful about using effective communication methods.

But if our goal is to catechize the next generation, we must do more than capture their eyes; we must capture their hearts. Doing so will involve more than grabbing their attention and then lecturing them about biblical truth. It will involve more than merely preaching the propositions and principles of Christian theology with engaging images. Our kids don't need the latest tech as much as they need an ancient path.

Our kids need to participate in church and family cultures where, by God's grace (1 Cor. 3:5–8), they can learn that what Christ offers is better than *Marvel*, *Star Wars*, or their favorite YouTube channel. They need cultures where thinking, affections, and patterns of life are captured and shaped by Jesus's redemptive story.

Reflection on Part 4

Grow with Kids and Families

TAKE A LOOK at the questions for reflection and evaluation below. Spend some time working through them and think about how you can help families take the next steps in their spiritual journeys.

Questions for Reflection and Evaluation

1. What practices could your children's ministry put in place to care for infants and toddlers who experience a fear of being separated from their parents? What are some practical ways that your ministry can model God's trustworthy care?

2. How would you manage a situation in which a five-year-old continues to act out by taking another child's toy? At what point would you involve a parent? What rules or classroom management techniques might you put in place to help teachers manage this type of situation?

3. How would you respond if a child in your ministry asks you about trusting Jesus? How would you encourage the child to confess his sin and express trust in Jesus? Role-play this interaction with a partner and then evaluate. Did the questions you asked encourage the child to see the sin and inconsistency in his heart? Did you explain the gospel clearly with age-appropriate language? Was your appeal for the child to trust Christ direct and clear?

4. What basic doctrines does your children's ministry curriculum emphasize? Why were these curriculum aims chosen? Would supplementing your curriculum with catechism memory help your teaching aims to be clearer?

5. What spiritual habits (times, moments, or milestones) would you like to see the families in your church develop? How could you encourage, celebrate, and model these habits for families?

For Further Study

On Catechism

DeYoung, Kevin. *The Good News We Almost Forgot: Rediscovering the Gospel in a 16th Century Catechism*. Chicago: Moody, 2010.

Johnson, Terry L. *The Family Worship Book: A Resource Book for Family Devotions*. Fearn, Ross-shire, Great Britain: Christian Focus, 1998. See pages 10–12, 61–93.

The New City Catechism for Kids. Wheaton, IL: Crossway, 2018.

The New City Catechism Curriculum. Edited by Melanie Lacy. Wheaton, IL: Crossway, 2018.

On Child Development

Bounds, Brent. "Train Up a Child: The Spiritual and Psychological Development of Children." Audio lecture. *Gospel in Life*, April 22, 2006, https://gospelinlife.com/downloads/train-up-a-child -the-spiritual-and-psychological-development-of-children/.

Henley, Karyn. *Child-Sensitive Teaching: Helping Children Grow a Living Faith in a Loving God*. 4th ed. Nashville: Child-Sensitive Communication, 2011.

On Family Discipleship

Chandler, Matt, and Adam Griffin. *Family Discipleship: Leading Your Home through Time, Moments, and Milestones*. Wheaton, IL: Crossway, 2020.

Hunt, Susan. *Heirs of the Covenant: A Biblical Legacy of Faith for All Generations*. Alpharetta, GA: Great Commission, 2014.

Jones, Timothy Paul. *Family Ministry Field Guide: How Your Church Can Equip Parents to Make Disciples*. Indianapolis: Wesley Publishing House, 2011.

Keeley, Robert J. *Helping Our Children Grow in Faith: How the Church Can Nurture the Spiritual Development of Kids*. Grand Rapids, MI: Baker, 2008.

Magruder, Jana. *Kids Ministry That Nourishes: Three Essential Nutrients of a Healthy Kids Ministry.* Nashville, TN: B&H Books, 2016.

PART 5

GO! SEND KIDS AND FAMILIES ON MISSION

Graceless Parents, Overly Spiritual Ministry, and Sticky Notes

Empowering Families with a
Gospel-Fueled Witness

ROBERT RAIKES of Gloucester, England, was born in 1736. He was a well-to-do man, inheriting the family business and expanding upon his father's property. But the younger Raikes didn't keep his wealth to himself. He used his prosperity in service of others, understanding his life as a part of God's larger mission.[1]

Raikes's philanthropy initially focused on prisoners incarcerated in the city's workhouse jails. By profession, Raikes was a newspaper writer and publicist, so he used both his pen and his purse to address the prisons' inhumane conditions. But as Raikes advocated for prisoners, he became convinced that the best way to fight high incarceration rates in Gloucester was to help underprivileged boys before they got into trouble. So, in 1780, he made what may have been his most lasting societal contribution. Robert Raikes invented Sunday school.[2]

During that time, children of poorer families had little schooling, and they often worked in factories alongside their parents six days each week, sometimes as much as twelve hours per day. Overburdened work schedules and a lack of access to education kept many families trapped in a cycle of poverty. And with many poorer parents imprisoned for petty crimes or exhausted after a long week's work, their kids would roam the streets on Sundays—gambling, cursing, and carousing.

That's where Raikes stepped in. He didn't merely see the street kids as a problem. He saw reaching them as an opportunity. Raikes recruited a local woman who could host and teach Sunday school classes in her home. The first Sunday school began with a focus on boys ages six to fourteen. The textbook was the Bible, and the originally intended curriculum started with learning to read and then progressed to learning the catechism. Instruction could last a full day—beginning at ten in the morning and stretching through church services, which ended after five in the evening.[3]

As the young boys learned the gospel, managers at the local pin factory where many of the boys worked noticed changes in their attitudes and behavior. Support for Raikes's efforts grew, and within two years, several Sunday schools opened in and around Gloucester. Not long after, Raikes was publicizing the schools through his newspaper, the *Gloucester Journal*, without mentioning that this was an operation that he had initially financed. Newspapers in London then picked up Raikes's story, and the idea of Sunday school soon became a movement. By 1850, Sunday schools had enrolled two million people across England.[4] What began with one man in 1780 who refused to live in isolation from the world's brokenness soon became a worldwide phenomenon.

We Are Invited to Join God on Mission

Over the course of this book, I've written about creating a strategic pathway for children's discipleship. But discipleship must move beyond the church and home. Christ commands us, "Go therefore and make disciples of all nations" (Matt. 28:19). So faith should move kids and families to be ambassadors for Christ who love their neighbors and take the good news to the world.

The truth is that the Great Commission isn't only something we're commanded to do. God himself was on mission long before he gave us this command. Theologian R. Paul Stevens says it this way: "Mission is God's own going forth. . . . He is Sender, Sent, and Sending."[5] The Father sent the Son (John 3:16–17; 5:36), the Father and Son send the Holy Spirit (John 14:26; 15:26), and now we are sent into the world (John 20:21; Acts 1:8).

In the New Testament, we see the sacrificial, gap-crossing character of God's mission in Jesus Christ. He was in very nature God, but he "did not consider equality with God something to be used to his own advantage; rather, he made himself nothing by taking the very nature of a servant" (Phil. 2:6–7 NIV).

In 2 Corinthians, Paul writes to tell us that the church's risk-taking ministry of reconciliation is rooted in what God has already accomplished: "In Christ God was reconciling the world to himself, not counting [the world's] trespasses against them" (5:19). As we experience this work of redemption, we join God on mission—controlled and empowered by his love to be gospel-fueled ambassadors to the world (5:18–20).

GOSPEL-FUELED WITNESS

Gospel-fueled witness—faith moves kids to be risk-taking, gap-crossing ambassadors for Christ who love their neighbors and take the good news to the world.

How can we encourage families to join God on mission? What does it look like to cultivate a risk-taking and courageous faith in the next generation? It begins with seeing the great gaps that we need to cross.

The Breaks in God's Storyline

If I'm honest, I have to admit that I tend toward a fractured way of looking at life and ministry. I tend to think that the mission of a Christian family and the mission of the church are two different things. But the Bible's storyline helps me to keep God's big mission in perspective.[6]

In chapter 1, I summarized the Bible's storyline as a fourfold movement: creation, fall, redemption, and consummation. This simple outline is pretty basic, but I struggle to believe that every part of the biblical message applies all the time. Often, I'm living as if the biblical storyline is broken in half. Here is what I mean.

Graceless and Isolated Families

As a dad, I'm proud of my daughters. It's easy to celebrate their dignity as girls who are made in God's image. I know that I'm responsible for protecting my children, teaching them to care for their bodies, and providing for them. And, because I see the ways my kids are sinful and weak, I'm quick to correct their behavior, to teach them what needs to change, and to help them make decisions that will lead to a more successful life.[7]

As parents, we tend to emphasize the first two movements in the Bible's storyline—creation and the fall—but we neglect the final two movements. We see our responsibility to provide for our children and correct their sins and imperfections, but we too easily miss our responsibility to be redemptive agents in their lives. When this happens, the family becomes merely a context for "behavior modification and personal success."[8]

When our perspective is limited to the first half of the storyline, we're in danger of diminishing even those movements. We tend to think that sin can be addressed by our own efforts. So, we'll regularly discipline, instruct, and encourage our children to pursue what is pure and good. We may even regularly share the gospel with our kids during family devotions or go beyond correcting misbehavior to shepherding our kids' heart motivations. But how often do we remember that the Bible's redemptive mission also involves confessing our own sin and repenting before our children as well? When we forget, we've become graceless.

Moreover, when our perspective is limited to the first half of the storyline, it's easy for our thinking to be isolated to our own family's needs, and we fail to give our children a vision for participating in God's larger mission.

Overly Spiritual Ministry

An equal but opposite temptation beguiles those of us who are in ministry. Because evangelism and discipleship are chief parts of our

Chart 10.1

The Broken Storyline[9]

CREATION FALL REDEMPTION CONSUMMATION

Graceless and Isolated Families

Family as a context for behavior modification and preparation for personal success.

When God's storyline is broken, parents receive the impression that their responsibilities end with providing for, protecting, and correcting their kids.

Parents miss their responsibility to be grace-filled redemptive agents in their children's lives, and they fail to give their children a vision for participating in God's mission.

Overly Spiritual Ministry

Church as a context for training and discipleship that is abstracted from the world's brokenness.

When God's storyline is broken, professional ministers at church can see themselves as elite fixers but are actually disconnected from the practical needs families in their churches face each day.

We can be aloof from the needs of the communities where we're planted, failing to see barriers that stand in the way of people coming to Christ.

job descriptions, we're tempted to embody the role of elite fixers. In the midst of preparing children's ministry lessons and crafting discipleship opportunities for families, we too easily forget just how hard it is for parents to live out the doctrines of redemption and consummation before their children when so many other things dominate their time.

Field hockey practice, allergy shots, car pool, and the school Christmas party—not to mention a sprained ankle, unemployment, or a broken marriage—tend to push ideal times of family discipleship to the side. If we lack awareness of the needs that families in our churches face each day, then the gospel we're preaching is overly spiritual, a message that's abstracted from embodied life in a broken world.

And an overly idealized and overly spiritual view of discipleship doesn't just keep ministers aloof from church families. It can also keep whole churches aloof from the needs of the communities where they are planted. When we fail to see the barriers that stand in the way of people coming to Christ, church can become a context for programmatic discipleship that's abstracted from the world's brokenness.

Praise God for a Savior who doesn't struggle with seeing ministry through only one or two parts of the biblical storyline. In Christ Jesus, God became man and lived among us. He united our beauty and brokenness in his flesh. He brought redemption, and, as the church joins him on mission, he's bringing about the renewal of all things.

A Reflection Activity with Sticky Notes

My prayer is that family ministries in our churches revive the gap-crossing, risk-taking spirit of Robert Raikes. I pray that we have more grounded ministry that helps leaders move from merely "running a department" or "leading a bunch of programs" to truly ministering to families in a way that better reflects the Savior's mission.

Authors Michelle Anthony and Megan Marshman have developed a reflection activity using sticky notes that I've adapted to help children's and family ministry leaders be more aware and intentional about the needs of families in their communities.[10] It has helped them to focus their ministry where it is needed. Here is how the activity works:

1. On a white board, write the words *Home* and *Church* side by side at the top of two columns with a clear gap in between.

2. Under *Home*, write the particular parts of the biblical story-line that are typically emphasized by parents, "Creation and Fall," as well as the danger, "graceless and isolated families," that we encounter when we focus on these parts of the storyline in isolation from the end of God's story.

3. Under *Church*, write the particular parts of the biblical story-line that are typically emphasized by pastors and ministry staff, "Redemption and Consummation," as well as the danger, "overly spiritualized ministry," that we encounter when we focus on these parts of the storyline in isolation from the beginning of the story. After you've completed these three steps, your white board should look something like chart 10.2.

4. Use yellow sticky notes to write down the various programs your local church offers for families. Include programs like vacation Bible school, small groups, family fun nights, family retreats, midweek programs, Sunday school, and youth camps. Use a different note for each program. Place these notes on the board under the word *Church*.

5. Then, use a second color of sticky notes—perhaps pink or green—to write down the practical needs and struggles that individual children and families in your community face on a regular basis. You should write down the fact that people are lost and need to hear the gospel. You may also write down struggles like depression and loneliness, divorce, drug and alcohol abuse, a lack of knowledge about the Bible, teenage pregnancy, poverty, apathy, and anger. Use a different note

Chart 10.2

Sticky Notes Reflection Activity

HOME	CHURCH
Emphasizes *creation* and *fall*	Emphasizes *redemption* and *consummation*
Danger: graceless and isolated families	Danger: overly spiritual ministry

for each need or struggle. Then, place these notes on the white board under the word *Home*. Think carefully about the particular needs of the families in your community. A leadership team in a rural church, a suburban church, and an urban church will likely write down different needs and struggles.

6. Draw a line from each yellow note to each of the needs that particular program meets or addresses. Circle any sticky notes that remain, and then work through the reflection questions I've included at the end of this chapter. When the activity is complete, it will look something like Chart 10.3, which you can find at the end of this chapter.

This activity can help your leadership team identify practical community needs that remain unmet by your ministry's current structure. God doesn't intend for our churches to meet every need that the families in our communities have. But becoming aware of these needs might reveal ways that you can encourage kids, parents, and children's ministry volunteers to step out of their comfort zones and join God on mission. The next step is to pray about which of these needs may be gospel opportunities for your church.

Joining God on Mission

It can be easy to live in isolation from the world's brokenness, but God calls us to step across the gap into the adventure of his mission. Here are two ways to help the kids and families in your church do just that:

First, teach kids about missions. In recent years, many churches have adopted simple programming structures, encouraging families to meet together weekly in small groups and sidelining Christian scouting programs like Awana that incorporate service projects, missionary testimonies, and some lessons about international language and culture. There are some advantages to this change. Children learn the faith from seeing it modeled intergenerationally, and families have more of an opportunity to be on mission in their communities. But there are disadvantages too. Even if the regular Sunday children's ministry curriculum covers the Great Commission and the expansion of the church in Acts, without programs that intentionally teach about service and mission, it's easy for kids to miss out on what God is doing around the world right now.

If you find yourself in this situation, be sure to make missions a regular part of your teaching plan. Pull out a missionary prayer card during the prayer time in your children's ministry classroom, set up a video chat with a missionary, or work with the kids to put together a care package for a missionary family that your church supports. Be certain that before kids leave your children's ministry, they know how God is at work around the world.

Second, create opportunities for families to get out of their comfort zones. I'm particularly thankful for some renewed ways that churches are living out Christ's more holistic ministry in our time. Renewed emphases on orphan care and ministry to refugees, for example, help us fight against a graceless and over-spiritualized life. Is your church active in efforts like these? If so, are you challenging the kids and families in your ministry to join these efforts?

Gather the kids to serve a local nursing home. Bring the teens along to serve with you at a homeless shelter or crisis pregnancy center. Help kids memorize the Scripture passages and gospel summary in an evangelistic booklet like my own *Are You Close to God?* (New Growth, 2015), and then encourage them to share their faith with a friend.

God transforms us when we step out in faith to join him on mission. I love how Anthony and Marshman describe it, "When children and students are challenged to step out of their comfort zones from an early age, they experience a dependence on the Spirit to equip and strengthen them beyond their nature and desires."[11]

The Great Commission runs in two directions—across geography and across time from generation to generation. Our prayer is that the next generation will be empowered by God's Spirit to reflect the kind of multi-cultural—every tribe and tongue—community we'll encounter when the kingdom comes (Rev. 7:9). May they be a generation that does not seek comfort but instead lives radical lives of faith in Christ. May they do justice, love mercy, and walk humbly with their God (Mic. 6:8). Lord, hear our prayer. Amen.

Chart 10.3

Completed Sticky Notes Reflection Activity

Home
What practical needs
and struggles do
children and families in
our community face?

Church
What programs does
our church offer?

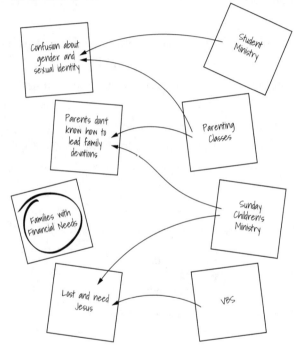

Reflection on Part 5

Go! Send Kids and Families on Mission

GRAB SOME STICKY NOTES and work through the reflection activity described in chapter 10. After you've completed it, think through the following reflection questions.

Questions for Reflection and Evaluation

1. How do you navigate any needs that are unmet by your current ministry structure (represented by the circled second-color notes)?

   Which unmet needs represent opportunities to encourage kids, parents, and children's ministry volunteers to step out of their comfort zones?

And which unmet needs reveal limits of your ministry—due to church size or limited financial and people resources—that you must honestly own? Owning limits is important; God's kingdom is always bigger than our ministries.

2. If God is calling your church to step into an area of need, how might you creatively meet that need? Could you adjust your teaching schedule to address this need? Could you partner with other ministry departments in your church, or other para-church ministries outside of your church to address this need?

3. As families step into areas of need in your community, are they prepared to share the gospel? Are you already challenging kids to invite their friends to church? Have you taught them to share their testimony? Have you given them clear resources to use when sharing the faith with their friends?

4. How are you educating the kids in your ministry about international missions? Does your church sponsor short-term mission trips where families can go on mission together? Does your children's ministry regular pray for or create care packages for

missionaries? What other ideas might help missions to be a regular part of your teaching?

5. Did you identify any programs that do not address specific needs of the families in your church or community (represented by the circled yellow notes)? Is it time to re-evaluate whether this program should continue?

For Further Study

Anthony, Michelle, and Megan Marshman. *7 Family Ministry Essentials: A Strategy for Culture Change in Children's and Student Ministries*. Colorado Springs: David C. Cook, 2015.

Dembowczyk, Brian. *Gospel Centered Kids Ministry: How the Gospel Will Transform Your Kids, Your Church, Your Community, and the World*. Nashville, TN: Lifeway, 2017.

Wall, Molly and Jason Mandryk, Eds. *Window on the World: An Operation World Prayer Resource*. Downers Grove, IL: IVP Books, 2018.

Conclusion

Courage for the Harvest

AS CHILDREN'S MINISTERS, there's perhaps nothing that tests our faith in God's provision quite like recruiting volunteers. When you've been told No several times over the course of a day, it can be discouraging.

I once participated in a conference call with a group of children's ministry leaders in our church's denomination. The topic of conversation was—you guessed it—recruiting teachers. The moderator asked, "What have you found to be most successful?" One leader piped up quickly, "I find the most success when I am the most *passionate and prayerful.*" That children's minister emphasized those last three words in his sentence, and it was convicting to me.

First, it's more likely that people will volunteer when they sense a leader's passion. One of my goals in this book has been to cultivate vision and excitement in you. It's tempting to look at your children's ministry schedules, see the needs for the upcoming month, and then rush into filling those gaps with anyone available.

But it's better to stop and think about *why* those volunteer roles are important.

Before approaching a perspective worker, meditate on the importance of reaching children with the gospel. Think about what you need to *create* welcoming environments, *connect* kids to Christ, *grow* alongside kids, and *go*, sending families on mission together. Remember that each role—from nursery to middle school, from greeter to assembly teacher—is essential to the mission. Then, you'll be ready to share your passion with potential volunteers.

Second, and more importantly, God has designed ministry so that it only moves forward when we depend on him—when we trust him and pray. In Matthew 9:36–38, we see how Jesus's vision moved him to compassion and then to prayer. He told his disciples, "The harvest is plentiful but the workers are few. Ask the Lord of the harvest, therefore, to send out workers into his harvest field" (NIV). This passage is a reminder for children's ministry leaders to ask specifically for God to bring to mind the names of individual people who are gifted for each needed role.

But it's also a reminder that we can ask with the courage and confidence of a patient farmer. You see, there's a promise in Jesus's words: "The harvest is plentiful!" Even if we can't see it right now, it's coming. So, we recruit volunteers and disciple children with courage, praying diligently for workers, for children to follow Christ by faith, and for families to grow in their affection for reading and obeying God's word. But when they do, we simply give thanks. You see, we certainly need workers to plow and plant and water, but ultimately God is the one who keeps children's ministry on mission. He is the one who gives the growth (1 Cor. 3:5–8).

Acknowledgments

IT TAKES A VILLAGE to raise a child. It's equally true that it takes a village to write a book. I'm so grateful for mine. Thank you to Ivan Mesa at The Gospel Coalition for advocating for this project and to Collin Hansen for helpful edits. Thanks to Todd Augustine and the team at Crossway for your diligent work in bringing this book to publication.

I'm grateful for the children's ministry leaders and volunteers of the Harbor Network and Sojourn Collective churches. The create-connect-grow-go model presented here began when Fletcher Lang and I started scribbling on a white board in Sojourn Community Church's Mary Street offices in 2010, and it was refined through a decade of service alongside and conversations with many of you.

Thanks to Joshua Cooley, Zach Cochran, Sam Luce, Champ Thornton, and Mark Smith for reading and giving feedback on chapters. Your skilled editing and invaluable encouragement pushed me along as I wrote.

Finally, my wife Megan read and edited every page. I'm so grateful for you, my beloved (Song 6:3). Thanks to all of my girls—Megan as well as Rachael, Lucy, and Elisabeth—for your patience when I had too much on my mind. Thank you for all of the happy interruptions during our family coronavirus quarantine, from playing games to watching Marvel movies and *The Mandalorian*.

May this book serve the church as we seek to raise generations that love Jesus. *Soli Deo gloria*.

Notes

Introduction

1. Jack Klumpenhower, *Show Them Jesus: Teaching the Gospel to Kids* (Greensboro, NC: New Growth, 2015), 15.
2. Categories adapted from Brian Dembowczyk, *Gospel-Centered Kids Ministry* (Nashville, TN: Lifeway, 2017). The definitions are adapted from Klumpenhower's exposition of 1 Corinthians 2:1–5 in *Show Them Jesus*, 14–16.

Chapter 1: Stop! Believe! Christ Sent Me.

1. Clement of Alexandria, "Who Is the Rich Man That Shall Be Saved?" in *The Ante-Nicene Fathers: Translations of the Writings of the Fathers Down to A.D. 325, Volume II, Fathers of the Second Century: Hermas, Tatian, Athenagoras, Theophilus, and Clement of Alexandria (Entire)*, ed. Alexander Roberts, James Donaldson, and Cleveland Coxe (repr., New York: Charles Scribner's Sons, 1905), 603. This translation of Clement is from Eusebius, *The Church History, A New Translation with Commentary*, trans. Paul L. Maier, 4th ed. (Grand Rapids, MI: Kregel, 1999), 111–12.
2. Tedd Tripp, "Session 14: Helping Kids See God's Glory," in *Case for Kids DVD* (Shepherd Press, 2006).
3. Robert L. Plummer, "Bring Them Up in the Discipline and Instruction of the Lord: Family Discipleship among the First Christians," in *Trained in the Fear of God: Family Ministry in Theological, Historical, and Practical Perspective*, eds. Randy Stinson and Timothy Paul Jones (Grand Rapids, MI: Kregel, 2011), 47.
4. Charles Spurgeon, *Come Ye Children* (London: Passmore and Alabaster, 1897), chapter 9, accessed online at https://archive.spurgeon.org/misc/cyc09.php.

5. Charles Spurgeon, *Come Ye Children*, chapter 9.

6. See Marty Machowski, *Leading Your Child to Christ: Biblical Direction for Sharing the Gospel* (Greensboro, NC: New Growth, 2012); and Graeme Goldsworthy, *Gospel-Centered Hermeneutics: Foundations and Principles of Evangelical Biblical Interpretation* (Downers Grove, IL: InterVarsity, 2006), 176–77.

7. Plummer, "Bring Them Up," 50.

8. Eusebius, *The Church History*, 111–12.

9. Clement of Alexandria, "Who Is the Rich Man That Shall Be Saved?" 603.

10. Reggie Joiner: *Think Orange: Imagine the Impact When Church and Family Collide* (Colorado Springs: David C. Cook, 2009), 85.

11. Adapted from Steve Wright and Christ Graves, *ApParent Privilege* (Wake Forest, NC: InQuest Publishing, 2008), 99–110.

12. Eusebius, *The Church History*, 112.

Chapter 2: Knowing What We Shouldn't Do

1. Jane E. Strohl, "The Child in Luther's Theology: 'For What Purpose Do We Older Folks Exist, Other Than to Care for . . . the Young?'" in *The Child in Christian Thought*, ed. Marcia J. Bunge (Grand Rapids, MI: Eerdmans, 2001), 139.

2. Timothy Paul Jones and Randy Stinson, "Family Ministry Models," in Michael and Michelle Anthony, *A Theology for Family Ministries* (Nashville, TN: B&H Academic, 2011), 159–60.

3. Martin Luther, "Lectures on Genesis, Chapters 21–25," in *Luther's Works*, 55 vols., ed. Jaroslav Pelikan (St. Louis: Concordia, 1955–1986), 4:384.

4. Martin Luther, "The Estate of Marriage" (1522), in *Luther's Works* 45:40–41.

5. Strohl, "The Child in Luther's Theology," 145.

6. Martin Luther, "The Small Catechism (1529)," in *Martin Luther's Basic Theological Writings*, ed. Timothy F. Lull (Minneapolis: Fortress, 1989), 471.

7. Luther's "The Small Catechism (1529)" was printed in both a German edition with headings "in the plain form in which the head of the family shall teach them to his household" and in a Latin edition "for the Use of Children in School. How, in a very Plain Form, Schoolmasters Should Teach . . . Their Pupils" (p. 476).

8. Timothy Paul Jones, "Historical Contexts for Family Ministry" in *Perspectives on Family Ministry*, 2nd ed. (Nashville, TN: B&H Academic, 2019), 29–30.

9. Jones, "Historical Contexts for Family Ministry," 33.

10. Jones, "Historical Contexts for Family Ministry," 37.

11. Timothy Paul Jones, *Family Ministry Field Guide: How Your Church Can Equip Parents to Make Disciples* (Indianapolis: Wesley, 2011), 83.

12. When Presbyterian pastor Mark DeVries wrote *Family-Based Youth Ministry* (Downers Grove, IL: InterVarsity, 1994), it was one of the first significant critiques of the youth ministry movement that presented a viable alternative.

13. Thirteen years after DeVries, pastor Voddie Baucham released *Family Driven Faith: Doing What It Takes to Raise Sons and Daughters Who Walk with God* (Wheaton, IL: Crossway, 2007). His book popularized the family-integrated approach.

14. Reggie Joiner, "Where Do You Start?" in *Collaborate: Family + Church*, ed. Michael Chanley (Louisville, KY: Ministers Label, 2010), 136. Joiner released his book, *Think Orange*, in 2009, and he argued for an integrated strategy that combined the influences of church and home. In the same year, Timothy Paul Jones and a group of church leaders released the first edition of *Perspectives on Family Ministry: 3 Views* (Nashville, TN: B&H Academic, 2009), which outlined the history of family ministry and gave names to each of the three approaches.

15. This chart adapted from Timothy Paul Jones, "Four Models for Family Ministry" (lecture, SBTS Regional Alumni Academy, St. Louis, MO, April 29, 2016).

16. Brandon Shields has written an excellent critique of the way these statistics were used by early proponents of the family ministry movement. See "Family-Based Ministry: Separated Contexts, Shared Focus" in *Perspectives on Family Ministry*, 2nd ed. (Nashville, TN: B&H Academic, 2019), 118–22.

17. Dave Harvey, "Lift the Heavy Burden of Shame: How to Care for Parents of Prodigals," Desiring God, August 21, 2017, https://www.desiringgod.org/articles/lift-the-heavy-burden-of-shame.

18. Russell Moore, *The Storm-Tossed Family: How the Cross Reshapes the Home* (Nashville, TN: B&H, 2018), 16–17.

19. Kevin Jones, "Responses to Paul Renfro," in *Perspectives on Family Ministry*, 2nd ed. (Nashville, TN: B&H Academic, 2019), 102.

20. Age-integrated, inter-generational house church meetings or small groups that meet in homes are one example. Such groups mix the generations without being an impediment to mission. Even in our daycare culture, unchurched parents seem to be more comfortable bringing their kids into someone else's home to share a meal and conversation with other families than they are asking their kids to sit quietly in a large public gathering week after week. I've also seen churches host larger family-integrated gatherings in an effective way. Some churches that regularly provide a nursery or children's ministry host a gathering with kid-friendly music and teaching on Good Friday and Christmas Eve.

21. Tim Chester and Steve Timmis, *Total Church: A Radical Reshaping around Gospel and Community* (Wheaton, IL: Crossway, 2008), 183.

Chapter 3: Meeting Jesus at the Front Door

1. Judith M. Gundry-Volf, "The Least and the Greatest: Children in the New Testament," in *The Child in Christian Thought*, ed. Marcia J. Bunge (Grand Rapids, MI: Eerdmans, 2001), 35.

2. See 2 Kings 2:23–24; Isa. 3:4; Prov. 4:13; 6:23; 16:22; 10:17; 19:18; 22:15; 23:12–14

3. Gundry-Volf, "The Least and the Greatest," 39.

4. Gundry-Volf, "The Least and the Greatest," 40.

5. D. A. Carson, "Matthew" in *Matthew, Mark, Luke* in *The Expositor's Bible Commentary*, ed. Frank E. Gaebelein, vol. 8 (Grand Rapids, MI: Zondervan, 1984), 397.

6. C. S. Lewis, *Mere Christianity*, in *The C. S. Lewis Signature Classics* (New York: Harper One, 2017), 107–8.

7. Sue Miller and David Staal, *Making Your Children's Ministry the Best Hour of Every Kid's Week* (Grand Rapids, MI: Zondervan, 2004), 66–69.

8. Virginia Ward, Reggie Joiner, and Kristen Ivy, *It's Personal: Five Questions You Should Answer to Give Every Kid Hope* (Cumming, GA: reThink Group, 2019), 38.

9. I've skipped over Matthew 18:6–9 in my exposition. The Savior's instructions there about protecting little ones from stumbling *is* an important part of gospel-seasoned hospitality that will be covered in chapter 4.

10. These ideas are adapted from Ward, Joiner, and Ivy, 26–29.

11. Though the reasons for this practice vary between Anglican, Lutheran, and Reformed churches. See Adam Harwood and Kevin E. Larson,

eds., *Infants and Children in the Church: Five Views on Theology and Ministry* (Nashville, TN: B&H Academic, 2017).

12. Robert J. Keeley, *Helping Our Children Grow in Faith: How the Church Can Nurture the Spiritual Development of Kids* (Grand Rapids, MI: Baker, 2008), 32–33. There's biblical evidence for this suggestion. In Hezekiah's time, even three-year-old Levites were given daily responsibilities in the Temple (2 Chron. 31:16).

13. Keeley, *Helping Our Children Grow in Faith*, 33–35.

14. Keeley, *Helping Our Children Grow in Faith*, 32. Kara E. Powell and Chap Clark's research through the Fuller Youth Institute described in *Sticky Faith: Everyday Ideas to Build Lasting Faith in Your Kids* (Grand Rapids, MI: Zondervan, 2011), chap. 5, confirms Keeley's observations: "The number one way that churches made the teens on our survey feel welcomed and valued was when the congregation showed an interest in them. More than any single program or event, adults making the effort to get to know the kids was far more likely to make the kids feel like a significant part of their church."

15. Gundry-Volf, "The Least and the Greatest," 41.

Chapter 4: Safety and Security in a Corrupted World

1. "Joe Paterno, Graham Spanier Removed," *ESPN.com*, November 9, 2011, https://www.espn.com/college-football/story/_/id/7214380/joe-paterno-president-graham-spanier-penn-state/.

2. D. A. Carson ("Matthew," in *Matthew, Mark, Luke* in *The Expositor's Bible Commentary*, ed. Frank E. Gaebelein, vol. 8 [Grand Rapids, MI: Zondervan, 1984], 398) and others argue on the basis of Matthew's usage of "little ones" in 10:42 that the humble or immature believer is in mind here rather than actual children, but if the child placed in the disciples' midst was still standing next to Jesus at this point in the story, then the qualifier "who believe in me" could also be taken to mean that Jesus is speaking specifically about believing children within the church (18:2). See Keith J. White, "'He Placed a Little Child in the Midst': Jesus, the Kingdom, and Children," in *The Child in the Bible*, eds., Marcia J. Bunge, Terence E. Fretheim, and Beverly Roberts Gaventa (Grand Rapids, MI: Eerdmans, 2008), 353–74.

3. Brent Bounds, "Train Up a Child: The Spiritual and Psychological Development of Children," audio lecture, posted by *Gospel in Life*, April 22, 2006, https://gospelinlife.com/downloads/train-up-a-child-the-spiritual-and-psychological-development-of-children/.

4. In *The Connected Child: Bring Hope and Healing to Your Adoptive Family* (New York: McGraw-Hill, 2007), Karyn B. Purvis, David R. Cross, and Wendy Lyons Sunshine explain, "Early deprivation and abuse can disrupt the way a growing child's body and brain develop, even the way the body produces and manages neurotransmitters. Infants who were abused before the age of two have enduring structural changes in the right hemisphere of their brain—which in turn affects their ongoing ability to cope with stress" (205–6). Cf. Brian Liechty, "Review of *The Connected Child* by K. B. Purvis, D. R. Cross, and W. L. Sunshine," *Journal of Biblical Counseling* 30, no. 3 (2016): 85–93.

5. Michael Weinreb, "Growing Up Penn State: The End of Everything at State College," November 16, 2011, *Grantland*, https://grantland .com/features/growing-penn-state/.

6. Cf. Isaiah 28:1; 29:1; 30:1.

7. Carson, "Matthew," 399.

8. One notorious example is the *Houston Chronicle's* "Abuse of Faith" series (February 10–June 6, 2019, https://www.houstonchronicle .com/local/investigations/abuse-of-faith/). Cf. Richard Hammar and Matthew Branaugh, "Protecting Youth in the #MeToo Era," webinar presented by *Church Law & Tax*, April 17, 2019, https://www.church lawandtax.com/web/2019/april/protecting-youth-in-metoo-era.html, and Deepak Reju, *On Guard: Preventing and Responding to Child Abuse at Church* (Greensboro, NC: New Growth, 2014), chapter 5.

9. Malcom Gladwell, *Talking to Strangers: What We Should Know about the People We Don't Know* (New York: Little, Brown, and Company, 2019), audiobook, chapter 5.

10. Reju, *On Guard*, 25–26.

11. Reju, *On Guard*, 26–27.

12. Hammar and Branaugh, "Protecting Youth in the #MeToo Era"; Reju, *On Guard*, 28–36.

13. Gladwell writes at length about this in *Talking to Strangers*, chapter 5; cf. Reju, *On Guard*, 20–21.

14. Diane Langberg, "Key Responses to Sexual Abuse: Hear from the Experts," in *Becoming a Church That Cares Well for the Abused Handbook*, ed. Brad Hambrick (Nashville, TN: B&H Publishing, 2019), 65–66.

15. Brad Hambrick, "Lesson 2 – Ministry Tension: Matthew 18 Complements (Doesn't Compete with) Romans 13" in *Becoming a Church That Cares Well*, 17.

16. Hambrick, "Lesson 2," 20.
17. See "Appendix A" in *Becoming a Church That Cares Well*, 181–282, which outlines the mandated reporting laws and relevant pastor-parishioner privilege statues for all fifty US states.
18. R. Albert Mohler Jr., "The Tragic Lessons of Penn State—A Call to Action," AlbertMohler.com, November 10, 2011, https://albertmohler .com/2011/11/10/the-tragic-lessons-of-penn-state-a-call-to-action. Our responsibility to report doesn't mean that restorative church discipline will not—at the right time—be an appropriate response to abuse as well. Following the law shouldn't keep us from acting in a redemptive way. In 1 Corinthians 6:9–11, Paul makes clear that those who continue to hide in sin will not enter God's kingdom. In his list of offenders, Paul includes some who would today fit the category of child sexual offenders. Then, he says, *"And such were some of you.* But you were washed, you were sanctified, you were justified in the name of the Lord Jesus Christ and by the Spirit of our God." Paul's statement is a reminder for us that gospel hope remains even for an abuser.

    Nevertheless, the resolution of a legal matter, a statement of repentance, and even acts of restitution on behalf of a perpetrator of physical or sexual abuse toward a child doesn't erase sin's consequences. Given the recidivism rates of registered sex offenders, a convicted person should never be allowed to work with children. And in many cases, perhaps most, a local church will not have adequate resources in place—security teams, counseling care, and discipleship avenues that are separated from potential victims—to allow an offender to continue attending church gatherings and programs. See Megan Fowler, "Sex Offenders Can Find Hope in Christ But Not Necessarily a Place at Church," *Christianity Today*, July 23, 2020, https://www.christianitytoday.com/news/2020 /july/sex-offender-welcome-church-abuse-safety-ministry.html; Roger Przybylski, "Recidivism of Adult Sex Offenders," *U.S. Department of Justice SOMAPI Research Brief*, July 2015, https://smart.ojp.gov /sites/g/files/xyckuh231/files/media/document/recidivismofadultsexual offenders.pdf; and Stephanie Smith, "Sex Offenders, Recidivism, and the Church," Religion News Service, July 25, 2014, https://religion news.com/2014/07/25/sex-offenders-recidivism-church/.

    If churches do welcome an offender into their care, they must be vigilant about following all legal restrictions and have a clear written care plan in place for any individual who has previously committed a crime against a child. The individual's willingness to submit to this plan will show whether or not his or her heart is repentant and teachable, and whether or not he or she is able to continue receiving the church's care. See Jared Kennedy, "12 Things to Consider When a Sex Offender Wants to Come to Church," Gospel-Centered Family, October 2019, https://gospelcenteredfamily.com/blog/12-things-to-consider-when-a-sex-offender-wants-to-come-to-church/.

19. Adapted from Brad Hambrick, "Lesson 2 – Ministry Tension: Matthew 18 Complements (Doesn't Compete with) Romans 13" in *Becoming a Church That Cares Well for the Abused Handbook*, ed. Brad Hambrick (Nashville, TN: B&H Publishing, 2019), 25.

20. Reju, *On Guard*, 49.

21. Reju, *On Guard*, 15. He cites Deuteronomy 10:18; Isaiah 1:17; Jeremiah 7:5–7; and James 1:27.

Reflection on Part 2: Create *Welcoming Environments*

1. Adapted from Michael S. Wilder and Timothy Paul Jones, *The God Who Goes before You: Pastor Leadership as Christ-Centered Followership* (Nashville, TN: B&H Academic, 2018), 79.

Chapter 5: Three Ways to Tell a Bible Story

1. "Little Guys Can Do Big Things Too," from *Veggie Tales: Dave and the Giant Pickle*, directed by Phil Vischer, (Lombard, IL: Big Idea Productions, 1996).

2. Jack Klumpenhower, *Show Them Jesus: Teaching the Gospel to Kids* (Greensboro, NC: New Growth, 2015), 102.

3. Sidney Greidanus, *Preaching Christ from the Old Testament: A Contemporary Hermeneutical Method* (Grand Rapids, MI: Eerdmans, 1999), 2–3.

4. Greidanus, *Preaching Christ*, 227–32.

5. Klumpenhower, *Show Them* Jesus, 101–24.

6. Adapted from Klumpenhower, *Show Them Jesus*, 102.

Chapter 6: The Proud King's Nightmare

1. Ernest C. Lucas, *Daniel*, Apollos Old Testament Commentary, no. 20 (Downers Grove, IL: InterVarsity, 2002), 114.

2. Jack Klumpenhower, *Show Them Jesus: Teaching the Gospel to Kids* (Greensboro, NC: New Growth, 2015), 102.

3. *The Reformation Study Bible* (2017), ed. R. C. Sproul (Sanford, FL: Reformation Trust, 2017); and *Biblical Theology Study Bible, NIV*, ed. D. A. Carson (Grand Rapids, MI: Zondervan, 2018).

4. Charles H. Spurgeon, "Christ Precious to Believers," sermon at Music Hall, Royal Surry Gardens, London, March 13, 1859.

Chapter 7: Hands-On, Real-Life, Engaging Discovery

1. Lawrence O. Richards and Gary J. Bredfeldt, *Creative Bible Teaching*, rev. and expanded ed. (Chicago: Moody Press, 1998), 290–91.

2. Richards and Bredfeldt, *Creative Bible Teaching*, 273–74; Also see the next chapter, which discusses stages of child development.

3. See the discussion of Bernice McCarthy's learning styles in Harro Van Brummelen, *Walking with God in the Classroom: Christian Approaches to Teaching and Learning*, 3rd ed. (Colorado Springs: Purposeful Design, 2009), 109–22; and Marlene D. Lefever, *Learning Styles: Reaching Everyone God Gave You to Teach* (Colorado Springs: NexGen/Cook, 2004), 19–35. See the discussion of Kolb's learning cycle in Michael J. Anthony, "Introduction: Putting Children's Spirituality in Perspective" in *Perspectives on Children's Spiritual Formation*, ed. Michael J. Anthony (Nashville, TN: B&H Academic, 2006), 36–43. For more about the HBLT method, see Lawrence O. Richards and Gary J. Bredfeldt, *Creative Bible Teaching* (Chicago: Moody Press, 1970, 1998), 151–65, 292–97.

4. LeFever, *Learning Styles*, 32, and Madison Michell, "Kinesthetic, Visual, Auditory, Tactile, Oh My! What Are Learning Modalities and How Can You Incorporate Them in the Classroom?" Edmentum, September 25, 2017, https://blog.edmentum.com/kinesthetic-visual -auditory-tactile-oh-my-what-are-learning-modalities-and-how-can -you-incorporate. Each chapter of LeFever's *Learning Styles* provides sample classroom activities listed by both learning style and modality.

5. Robert J. Keeley, *Helping Our Children Grow in Faith: How the Church Can Nurture the Spiritual Development of Kids* (Grand Rapids, MI: Baker, 2008), 74–75.

6. See, for example, the explanation of "Bible Time" (p. 10) and some of the sample Bible stories in *Show Me Jesus! Toddler (Ages 2–3): Winter, God's Son* (Alpharetta, GA: Great Commission, 1999).

7. Catherine F. Vos, *The Child's Story Bible*, rev. by Marianne Catherine Vos Radius, 5th ed. (Grand Rapids, MI: Eerdmans, 1985); Sally Lloyd-Jones, *The Jesus Storybook Bible* (Grand Rapids, MI: ZonderKidz, 2007); and Jared Kennedy, *The Beginner's Gospel Story Bible* (Greensboro, NC: New Growth, 2017).

8. *Show Me Jesus! Toddler*, 10.

9. I'm grateful for the Gospel-Centered Family Fall 2020 Children's Ministry Leadership Cohort for helping me come up with some of the activities throughout this chapter.

10. *The New City Catechism: 52 Questions and Answers for Our Hearts and Minds* (Wheaton, IL: Crossway, 2017); *The New City Catechism for Kids* (Wheaton, IL: Crossway, 2018).

11. Stephanie Carmichael, *Their God Is So Big: Teaching Sunday School to Young Children* (Kingsford NSW, Australia: Matthias Media, 2000), 72.

12. Carmichael, *Their God Is So Big*, 76.

13. Dave made this observation to me while we were talking through the material for this chapter. I'm grateful for his permission to quote him.

Chapter 8: Step-by-Step, Stage-by-Stage

1. Douglas Davies, *Child Development: A Practitioner's Guide*, 3rd ed. (New York: Guilford, 2011), 162.

2. Adapted from Davies, *Child Development*, 160–62, 222–24.

3. Brent Bounds, "Train Up a Child: The Spiritual and Psychological Development of Children," audio lecture, *Gospel in Life*, April 22, 2006, https://gospelinlife.com/downloads/train-up-a-child-the-spiritual-and-psychological-development-of-children/.

4. Karyn Henley, *Child Sensitive Teaching: Helping Children Grow a Living Faith in a Loving God*, rev. ed. (Nashville, TN: Child Sensitive Communication, 2002), 35–36.

5. Richard Plass and James Cofield, *The Relational Soul: Moving from False Self to Deep Connection* (Downers Grove, IL: InterVarsity, 2014), 26–30.

6. I love how Sally Michael's curriculum, *A Sure Foundation: The Fragrance of the Knowledge of Christ, A Philosophy for Infant Nursery Ministry* (Minneapolis: Children Desiring God, 2005), cultivates this culture through simple stories and blessing prayers.

7. Karyn Henley, *Child Sensitive Teaching*, 41.

8. Adapted from *Show Me Jesus! Toddler*, 17; Davies, *Child Development*, 222–24; and Julie Lowe, "Counseling Children of Different Age Groups: Ages and Stages of Development," in *Caring for the Souls of Children: A Biblical Counselor's Manual*, ed. Amy Baker (Greensboro, NC: New Growth, 2020), 37–38.

9. *Show Me Jesus! Toddler*, 17.

10. Daniel J. Siegel, *The Developing Mind: How Relationships and the Brain Interact to Shape Who We Are*, 2nd ed. (New York: Guilford, 2012), 56.

11. Adapted from Davies, *Child Development*, 300–3, and Lowe, "Counseling Children of Different Age Groups," 39–41.

12. Mark Smith, "3 Key Truths to Teach Your Kids about the Conscience," October 14, 2020, Ethics and Religious Liberty Commission, https://erlc.com/resource-library/articles/3-key-truths-about-the-conscience-to-teach-your-kids/.

13. Charles E. Schaefer and Theresa Foy DiGeronimo, *Ages & Stages: A Parent's Guide to Normal Childhood Development* (New York: Wiley, 2000), 185.

14. Adapted from Lowe, "Counseling Children of Different Age Groups," 42–47, and Schaefer and DiGeronimo, *Ages & Stages*, 165–220.

15. Lowe, "Counseling Children of Different Age Groups," 43.

16. Adapted from "The Complete Plan to Teach God's Complete Word," 2019, Great Commission Publications, https://www.gcp.org/Downloads/TeachingGodsCompletePlan.pdf.

Chapter 9: Catechizing the YouTube Generation

1. Alisa Childers, "Let's Deconstruct a Deconversion Story: The Case of Rhett and Link," The Gospel Coalition, February 29, 2020, https://www.thegospelcoalition.org/article/rhett-link-deconversion/.

2. Childers, "Deconstruct a Deconversion."

3. Scottie May, "What Have We Learned? Seventy-Five Years of Children's Evangelical Spiritual Formation" in *Bridging Theory and Practice in Children's Spirituality*, ed. Mimi L. Larson and Robert J. Keeley (Grand Rapids, MI: Zondervan Reflective, 2020), 21–38.

4. Adapted from the excellent exposition of this passage in Susan Hunt, *Heirs of the Covenant: Leaving a Legacy of Faith for the Next Generation* (Wheaton, IL: Crossway, 1998), 143–49.

5. The next several paragraphs about catechism are adapted from an article I co-authored with my friend Sam Luce entitled, "Kids Have Questions. Do You Have an Answer?" in *K! Magazine* (May/June 2011), 54–57.

6. The earliest such summary we have today is *The Didache*, a manuscript that is older than some of the books included in the Bible.

7. Dorothy L. Sayers, "The Lost Tools of Learning" (academic paper, Oxford, UK, 1947), 13, https://www.pccs.org/wp-content/uploads/2016/06/LostToolsOfLearning-DorothySayers.pdf.

8. The two most famous and widely accepted Protestant catechisms, *The Heidelberg Catechism* (1576) and the *Westminster Shorter Catechism* (1642–47), follow this structure as well.

9. Aaron Earls, "Catching Some Z's: How the Church Can Reach the Most Connected and Distracted Generation Ever," Lifeway Research, September 29, 2017, https://lifewayresearch.com/2017/09/29/genz -single-page/.

10. Amanda Lenhart, "Teens, Social Media, and Technology Overview 2015," Pew Research Center, April 9, 2015, https://www.pew research.org/internet/2015/04/09/teens-social-media-technology -2015/.

11. Danah Boyd, "Why Youth (Heart) Social Network Sites: The Role of Networked Publics in Teenage Social Life," in *Youth, Identity, and Digital Media Volume*, ed. David Buckingham, MacArthur Foundation Series on Digital Learning (Cambridge, MA: MIT Press, 2007), https://www.danah.org/papers/WhyYouthHeart.pdf.

12. Champ Thornton, "How to Raise Radical Children," The Gospel Coalition, February 6, 2017, https://www.thegospelcoalition.org/article /how-to-raise-radical-children/.

13. Allen Curry, "Drawing a Bead on Curriculum" (Norcross, GA: Great Commission), cited in Hunt, *Heirs of the Covenant*, 170–72.

14. Bob Smietana, "Young Bible Readers More Likely to Be Faithful Adults, Study Finds," Lifeway Research, October 17, 2017, https:// lifewayresearch.com/2017/10/17/young-bible-readers-more-likely-to -be-faithful-adults-study-finds/.

15. James K. A. Smith, *Desiring the Kingdom: Worship, Worldview, and Cultural Formation*, Cultural Liturgies, vol. 1 (Grand Rapids, MI: Baker Academic, 2009), 32–33.

16. Matt Chandler and Adam Griffin, *Family Discipleship: Leading Your Home through Time, Moments, and Milestones* (Wheaton, IL: Crossway, 2020), 43.

17. Chandler and Griffin, *Family Discipleship*, 43.

Chapter 10: Graceless Parents, Overly Spiritual Ministry, and Sticky Notes

1. "The Memoir of Robert Raikes," *The Belfast Monthly Magazine* 7, no. 41 (December 31, 1811): 459–66, https://www.jstor.org/stable /30074425; Aaron Earls, "How the Forgotten History of Sunday School Can Point the Way Forward," Facts & Trends, July 17, 2018, https://factsandtrends.net/2018/07/17/sunday-school/.

2. "Memoir of Robert Raikes." W. Ryan Steenburg with Timothy Paul Jones, "Growing Gaps from Generation to Generation: Family Discipleship in Modern and Postmodern Contexts," in *Trained in the*

Fear of God: Family Ministry in Theological, Historical, and Practical Perspective (Grand Rapids, MI: Kregel Academic, 2011), 147–48.

3. Montrose J. Moses, *Children's Books and Reading* (New York: Mitchell Kennerly, 1907), 103, accessed online at https://www.google.com /books/edition/Children_s_Books_and_Reading/vqkaAAAAMAAJ.

4. Earls, "How the Forgotten History of Sunday School Can Point the Way Forward."

5. R. Paul Stevens, *The Other Six Days: Vocation, Work, and Ministry in Biblical Perspective* (Grand Rapids, MI: Eerdmans, 2000), 194.

6. Timothy Paul Jones, *Family Ministry Field Guide: How Your Church Can Equip Parents to Make Disciples* (Indianapolis: Wesley, 2011), 72.

7. Jones, *Family Ministry Field Guide*, 85

8. Jones, *Family Ministry Field Guide*, 85.

9. Adapted from Jones, *Family Ministry Field Guide*, 85, 113.

10. Michelle Anthony and Megan Marshman, *7 Family Ministry Essentials: A Strategy for Culture Change in Children's and Student Ministries* (Colorado Springs: David C. Cook, 2015), 30–31.

11. Anthony and Marshman, *7 Family Ministry Essentials*, 61.

General Index

Page numbers in italics indicate a chart.

Scripture Index

TGC | THE GOSPEL COALITION

The Gospel Coalition (TGC) supports the church in making disciples of all nations, by providing gospel-centered resources that are trusted and timely, winsome and wise.

Guided by a Council of more than 40 pastors in the Reformed tradition, TGC seeks to advance gospel-centered ministry for the next generation by producing content (including articles, podcasts, videos, courses, and books) and convening leaders (including conferences, virtual events, training, and regional chapters).

In all of this we want to help Christians around the world better grasp the gospel of Jesus Christ and apply it to all of life in the 21st century. We want to offer biblical truth in an era of great confusion. We want to offer gospel-centered hope for the searching.

Join us by visiting TGC.org so you can be equipped to love God with all your heart, soul, mind, and strength, and to love your neighbor as yourself.

TGC.org

The New City Catechism
Curriculum Kit

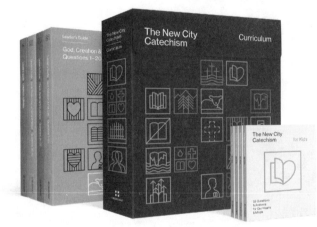

The New City Catechism Curriculum expands the questions and answers of the New City Catechism into 52 engaging and informative lessons, helping children ages 8–11 better understand the truth of God's Word and how it connects to their lives.

For more information, visit **newcitycatechism.com**.